Silas Farmer

Guide and souvenir of Detroit

With map and illustrations

Silas Farmer

Guide and souvenir of Detroit
With map and illustrations

ISBN/EAN: 9783742892614

Manufactured in Europe, USA, Canada, Australia, Japa

Cover: Foto ©Andreas Hilbeck / pixelio.de

Manufactured and distributed by brebook publishing software (www.brebook.com)

Silas Farmer

Guide and souvenir of Detroit

PORTRAIT OF
MAJOR GENERAL ANTHONY WAYNE
AFTER WHOM
WAYNE COUNTY WAS NAMED.

The Wayne County Savings Bank
HAS A GOOD NAME.

Original Bounds
of
WAYNE COUNTY.

ORGANIZED AUGUST 15, 1796.

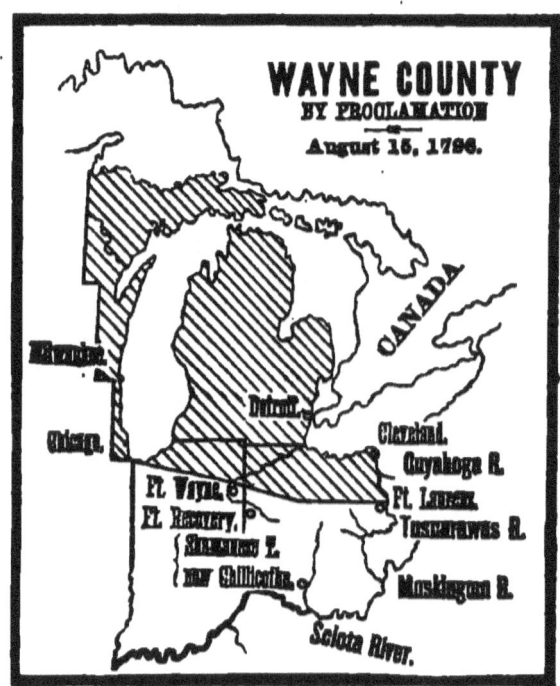

The Wayne County Savings Bank

WAS ORGANIZED OCTOBER 2, 1871.

Guide and Souvenir

OF

DETROIT

WITH

MAP AND ILLUSTRATIONS

BY

SILAS FARMER

Historiographer of the City of Detroit

Author of "History of Detroit and Michigan" "The Royal Rail Road"
"The Teacher's Tool Chest" etc., etc.

PUBLISHED BY

SILAS FARMER & CO.

31 Monroe Avenue, Corner of Farmer Street,
Detroit, Mich.

INDEX.

Advantages of Detroit, 44, 46.
Art Museum, 12.
Ann Arbor, 78.
Athletic Clubs, 46.
Bagley Fountain and Bust, 2.
Banks, 82.
Bank Capital, 52.
Bank Proverbs, 88.
Belle Isle Park, 16, 32, 34.
Belle Isle Bridge, 16, 34.
Belt Line Railroad, 68.
Biddle House, 12.
Board of Trade, 52.
Boat Houses, 12.
Boating Facilities, 48.
Boulevard, 34.
Brush Street Depot, 12.
Catholic Cathedral, now SS. Peter and Paul's Church, 12.
Canadian Pacific R. R. Depot, 28.
Canal St. Clair Flats, 80.
Campus Martius, 2.
Capuchin Church and Monastery, 16.
Carriages, 70.
Cass Ave. Baptist Church, 6.
Cass Ave. Methodist Episcopal Church, 8.
Census of City, 44.
Census of Wayne County, 36.
Central M. E. Church, 6.
Custom House, 26.
Chathâm, 80.
Charities, Amount Invested in, 44.

Christ Episcopal Church, 12.
Churches, No. of, 44.
City Hall, 1.
City Seal, 35.
Clock in City Hall, 1.
Convent of Good Shepherd, 28.
College Jesuit, 12.
College Detroit Medical, 20.
Detroit Athletic Club, 8.
Detroit College of Medicine, 20.
Detroit, Lansing & Northern R. R. Depot, 28.
Detroit & Milwaukee R. R. Depot, 12.
Deposits in Wayne County Bank, 53.
Depots, 12, 18, 28.
District Telegraph Co., 72.
Drives Carriage, 32.
Emigration in 1880, 40.
Epiphany Reformed Episcopal Church, 24.
Evening Journal, 26.
Evening News, 28.
Exposition Buildings, 30.
Families, Number of, 44.
Fire of 1805, 35.
Fire Com. Offices, 28.
Fire Department Facilities, 44.
First Congregational Church, 8.
First Presbyterian Church, 8.
Fishing and Hunting, 80.
Ferries, 68.
Ferry's Seed Warehouse, 20.
Ferry's Seed Farms, 24.

INDEX.

Flint & Pere Marquette R. R. Depot, 28.
Fort and River Streets, 28 to 30.
Fort Shelby, 28, 40.
Fort Street Bridge, 28.
Fort Street Presbyterian Church, 28.
Fort Wayne, 30.
Free Press, 28.
French Farms, 35, 42.
Gas Works, 12.
Grace Episcopal Church, 28.
Grace Hospital, 8.
Grand River Avenue, 24, 26.
Grand Trunk Junction, 26.
Grand Circus Park, 6.
Grant's Old Home, 18.
Gratiot Avenue, 20, 24.
Good Shepherd Convent, 28.
Griswold Street, 26, 28.
Grosse Pointe, 18.
Grotto of Virgin Mary, 22.
Hack Fares, 70.
Halls and Opera Houses, 74.
Harper Hospital, 8.
Hamtramck's Grave, 14.
Hamtramck House, 18.
Historical Sketch, 35, 52.
Home of the Friendless, 8.
Hotels, 72, 80.
House and Store Numbers, 60, 62.
House of Correction, 20.
Hunting and Fishing, 48
Immanuel Lutheran Church, 26.
Industrial School, 24.
Insane Asylum, 78.
International Exposition, 30.
Irving School, 8.
Jefferson Avenue, 10, 18.

Jefferson Avenue Presbyterian Church, 12.
Jesuit College, 12.
John Brown House, 18.
Junction, Grand Trunk, 26.
Lake Erie, Essex & Detroit River R. R., 80.
Lake St. Clair, 1, 46.
Lake Shore & Mich. Southern R. R. Depot, 12.
Little Sisters' Home, 22.
Lunch Rooms, 74.
Lyceum Theatre, 20.
Magnetic Springs, 80.
Manufacturing Institutions, 50.
Marine Hospital, 14.
Messenger Service, 72.
Mettawas Hotel, 80.
Michigan Avenue, 26.
Mich. Central R. R. Depot, 18.
Mt. Clemens, 80.
Mt. Elliott Cemetery, 14.
Municipal Courts, 20.
Musical Advantages, 50.
Museum of Art, 48.
Normal School, 78.
North Baptist Church, 10.
Oakland Hotel, 80.
Orchard Lake, 78.
Opera Houses and Halls, 74.
Orphan Asylum, Catholic, 14.
Orphan Asylum, Protestant, 14.
Our Lady of Help, Catholic Church, 14.
Palmer's Log House, 10.
Pontiac, 78.
Perry's Cave, 78.
Police Force, 44.
Police Headquarters, 20.
Polish Cathedral, 22.

INDEX.

Pontiac Tree, 14.
Population of City, 44.
Population of Wayne County, 36.
Post Office, 26.
Public Library, 4.
Public Schools, 44.
Put-in-Bay, 78.
River and Islands, 74, 76.
River Thames, 80.
Rail Road Bridge, 12.
Rail Road Depots, 72.
Rail Road Ferries, 18.
Sacred Heart Academy, 12.
Safe Deposit Co., 84.
Second Avenue Presbyterian Church, 24.
Simpson M. E. Church, 24.
Soldiers' Monument, 2.
Star Island, 78.
Steamboat Lines, 68, 70.
Streets Early, 35,
Street Rail Roads, 62, 64, 66.
St. Anne's Catholic Church, 28.
St. Boniface Catholic Church, 26.
St. Clair Flats, 80.
St. John's Episcopal Church, 6.
St. John's Lutheran Church, 20.
St. Joseph's Episcopal Church, 10.
St. Luke's Hospital, 30.
St. Mary's Hospital, 20.
St. Patrick's Catholic Church, 6.
St. Peter's Episcopal Church, 26.
St. Vincent de Paul Catholic Church, 26.
Steamboat Lines, 70.
Taxable Valuations, 44.
Taxes, City when payable, 54, 56.
Taxes, State and County when payable, 58, 59.
Telegraph Offices, 26, 72.
Thames River, 80.
Thompson Home for Old Ladies, 8.
Thompson Presbyterian Church, 10.
Trumbull Avenue Presbyterian Church, 24.
Unitarian Church, 6.
University of Michigan, 78.
Universalist Church, 6.
View from City Hall Tower 1.
Wabash & St. Louis R. R. Depot, 28.
War with South, 40.
Water Commission Offices, 12.
Water Works Reservoir, 18.
Walkerville, 80.
Walkerville Ferry, 12.
Wayne County Savings Bank, 38, 53, 82.
Whitney's Opera House, 28.
Woodmere Cemetery, 30.
Woodward Avenue 4, 10.
Woodward Ave. Baptist Church, 6.
Woodward Ave. Congregational Church, 6.
Woodward Ave. M. E. Church, 10.
Westminster Presbyterian Church, 8.
Woodward Avenue Railroad Station, 10.
Young Men's Christian Association, 6, 74.
Young Woman's Home, 6.
Ypsilanti, 78.

ILLUSTRATIONS.

Art Museum, 43.
Boat House, Belle Isle Park, 109.
Casino, Belle Isle Park, 108.
Central M. E. Church, 19.
Christ Episcopal Church, 45.
City Hall, 3.
Elmwood Cemetery, Views in, 49.
Engine House, 17.
First Presbyterian Church, 27.
Fort Shelby, 95.
Fort St. Presbyterian Church, 97.
Grace Hospital, 31.
Gen. Grant's Old Home, 63.
Grosse Pointe, 61.
Grotto of the Virgin, 91.
Harper Hospital, 29.
High School, 11.
Home of the Friendless, 39.
House of Correction, Main Building, 81.
House of Correction, Superintendent's Residence, 83.
Irving School, 33.
John Brown House, 65.
Little Sisters Home for Aged Poor, 89.
Marine Hospital, 55.
Market Building, 7.
Medical College Detroit, 77.
Mich. Central R. R. Depot, 67.
Monument Soldiers, 5.
Mount Elliott Cem. Entrance, 57.
Municipal Courts Building, 73.
Police Headquarters, 71.
Pontiac Tree, 51.

Post Office, 93.
Public Library, 13.
Railroad Bridge Jefferson Ave., 47.
Railroad Ferry Dock, 69.
Seal of City, 34.
Soldiers' Monument, 5.
St. Anne's Catholic Church, 99.
St. John's Lutheran Church, 79.
St. John's P. E. Church, 21.
St. Luke's Hospital, 103.
St. Mary's Hospital, 75.
St. Peter and Paul Catholic Church, 41.
Thompson Home for Old Ladies, 37.
Unitarian Church, 25.
Vaults of Safe Deposit Co., 85, 86, 87.
Vegetable Market, 9.
Water Works, 59.
Wayne Co. Bank, Exterior of, inside back cover.
Wayne Co. Bank, Interior of, 114.
Wayne County, Map of. ix.
Wayne Co., Original Bounds of, i.
Wayne, Portrait of General, inside front cover.
Windmill Point, 101.
Woodmere Cemetery Entrance, 105.
Woodward Ave. Baptist Church, 23.
Young Men's Christian Association, 15.

MAP OF
Wayne County, Mich.
AS NOW ORGANIZED.

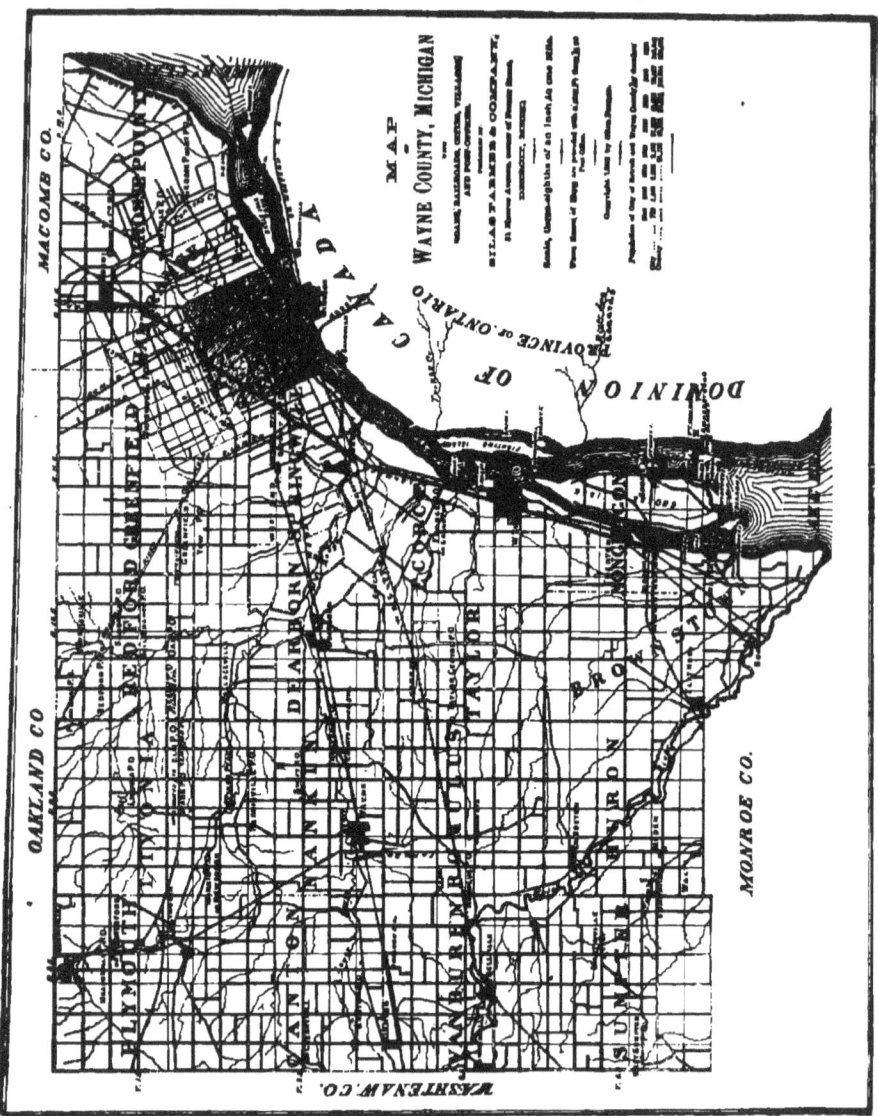

An Itinerary for Detroit.

A View from the City Hall Tower.

The most comprehensive view of the city can be obtained by ascending to the tower of the City Hall. Take a field glass with you, and from the windows you will see sights that will well repay for the time taken.

The whole city, river and islands, and even Lake St. Clair, five miles away, like a panorama will lie before you, and each window, in turn, will reveal beauties of its own.

The City Hall.

The City Hall itself, was erected at a cost of $600,000, and the ground is valued at perhaps twice as much more.

The City took formal possession of the building on July 4, 1871. Its size is 90x200 feet. Its height to cornice, 66 feet, and to top of flag-staff, 200 feet. The four stone figures about the tower are each 14 feet high, and represent Justice, Industry, Art and Commerce.

The clock is the largest in the United States, and there is but one larger in the world. It cost $3,000, and is wound up weekly. The dials are $8\frac{1}{4}$ feet in diameter. The four statues at the four corners in the second story, represent Cadillac, the founder of Detroit, Father Richard, an early local priest, La Salle, one of the earliest French explorers, and Father Marquette, one of the first Jesuit missionaries. The statues were presented to the City by Bela Hubbard, and were placed in position in August, 1884.

Campus Martius and Vicinity.

Coming down from the tower, the Soldiers' Monument, directly in front of the City Hall, will next claim your attention. It was designed by Randolph Rogers, and erected at a cost of $70,000. It was formally unveiled and dedicated on April 9, 1872. The monument is designed as an offering to the memory of the brave men from Michigan who perished in the war with the South, and bears the following inscription: "ERECTED BY THE PEOPLE OF MICHIGAN, IN HONOR OF THE MARTYRS WHO FELL AND THE HEROES WHO FOUGHT IN DEFENCE OF LIBERTY AND UNION."

The body of the monument is of Westerly, Rhode Island, granite, and the statues are of golden bronze, cast in Munich, Bavaria. The general design of the monument is embraced in four sections. The first section has, at its corners, four bronze eagles. The second section has four statues, representing the four departments of the United Service,—Infantry, Marine, Cavalry, and Artillery; each of the statues is seven feet high. The third section has four allegorical figures, representing Victory, Union, Emancipation, and History. The fourth section, or crowning figure of the monument, is eleven feet high, and represents Michigan allegorically, in aboriginal garb. On the four sides of the monument are bronzed medallions of Lincoln, Grant, Farragut, and Sherman. The height of the monument, including the crowning figure, is sixty feet. On the left of the monument is a bronze bust of Ex-Governor John J. Bagley erected at a cost of about $1,500, by popular subscriptions, and on the right in the centre of Fort street is the Bagley Fountain erected at a cost of $5,000 in pursuance of a bequest by Mr. Bagley. Immediately in the rear of the monument is the Central Market building in the second story of which are the

THE CITY HALL.

offices of the Park Commission and the Board of Health, and in the rear of the building, the vegetable market.

On the left, or north of the monument, and also facing the Campus Martius, which has few or no equals elsewhere as a public square, is the Detroit Opera House; a really elegant structure, capable of seating 2,000 persons.

Going up Woodward Avenue one block to State Street, and turning to the left one block, at the north end of Griswold Street, the large and imposing High School looms into view. One block from Woodward Avenue to the right you will find the Public Library, a large and substantial building, erected at a cost of $156,000, and dedicated January 22, 1877. It stands in the centre of a triangular park and contains about 100,000 volumes. Connected with it there is a very large and exceptionally well lighted free reading room, which is liberally supplied with current periodicals and newspapers, at an expenditure of nearly a thousand dollars per year. The Library is free to any person for consultation, and any resident of Detroit over fifteen years of age may draw books, after signing an agreement to abide by the rules, and getting some citizen to sign as surety. In the second story there is quite an extensive free museum which is well worthy of a visit.

Woodward Avenue.

This avenue is *par excellence* the avenue of the city, with one terminus at the river's edge, and the other reaching in a straight line for an indefinite distance into the country. Of an unusual width, and with an ever increasing number of the most elegant stores and residences along its route, it is probably excelled by no avenue on the continent. It stands as a type of progressive American ideas and is eminently modern and stylish.

THE SOLDIERS' AND SAILORS' MONUMENT.

Returning to this avenue, and going one block northwards, you will see on the left at the corner of Grand River Avenue and Griswold Street, the imposing and elegant building of the Young Men's Christian Association, one of the very finest structures of the kind in the world, and it will well repay you to inspect its interior arrangements. One block further north at the head of Clifford Street is one of the best of the fire engine houses.

Taking the Woodward Avenue line of street cars, and proceeding a few blocks northward, you will see on either side the Grand Circus Parks; their fountains and the seats inviting to rest and meditation. Here, especially on a summer evening, large numbers of children and adults gather to enjoy the cool of the day and the pleasing scenes. Fronting on the West Park is the elegant Universalist Church, built of stone and known as the Church of Our Father.

On the right of Woodward Avenue, immediately after leaving the Grand Circus, is the large and costly stone church, chapel and parsonage of the Central M. E. Church, and on the left, two blocks away, the Young Woman's Home, an attractive and substantial building. Three blocks further on the right of Woodward Avenue, are the beautiful buildings of St. John's Episcopal Church, including church, chapel, rectory and church house. Soon after, on the right, you pass the handsome church and chapel of the Woodward Avenue Baptist Church. A block further, on the left, is the Woodward Avenue Congregational Church, and on the right, one block away, at the corner of Adelaide and John R Streets, is St. Patrick's Roman Catholic Church. At Bagg Street, looming up through the trees, and two blocks away, on the left, you will see the tower of the Cass Avenue Baptist Church, while on the right at Edmund Street is the Unitarian Church, and on the opposite side of Edmund Street the elegant, brown

THE CENTRAL MARKET BUILDING.

stone edifice of the First Presbyterian Church. A number of blocks further on, you will notice on the left the round brick tower of the Westminster Presbyterian Church, and a block further and one block from Woodward Avenue on the left, on the corner of Cass and Selden Avenues, is the Cass Avenue M. E. Church, and a block away on the right at John R Street, the ample grounds and commodious building of Harper Hospital, named after its founder, Walter Harper, but largely endowed also by a former well-known market woman, Nancy Martin. On the same street, at the corner of Willis Avenue two blocks further north, is Grace Homœopathic Hospital named after a daughter of Senator James McMillan, who was the chief founder of this helpful institution. At Willis Avenue also, just off from Woodward Avenue on the left, is the Irving Public School, a good sample of the school buildings of the city. Immediately after passing Willis and Canfield Avenues, you will see on the left the large arched doorways of the Detroit Athletic Club House, used by one of the largest and best patronized clubs in the city. Two blocks further, at Forest Avenue on the right, is one of the latest and most beautiful of churches, the First Congregational. Four blocks north and one block west at the corner of Cass and Hancock Avenues is the Thompson Home for Old Ladies; named after its largest benefactor, Mrs. David Thompson. It is one of the most beautiful and beneficial of the local charities.

The next place of public interest is the large and well arranged building known as the "Home of the Friendless," situated on Warren Avenue, just off Woodward, on the left. Go in, if you have time, and you will be more thankful that such broad and benevolent institutions have an existence. Returning to Woodward Avenue and passing a continual succession of increasingly beautiful residences,

THE VEGETABLE MARKET.

just off from Woodward on Hendrie Avenue you will see the chapel of the Thompson Presbyterian Church. A few blocks further on the right at Medbury Avenue is the chapel of St. Joseph's Protestant Episcopal Church, and soon after you will also pass on the right the chapel of the Woodward Avenue Methodist Episcopal Church.

A ride of three miles from the City Hall brings you to the railroad crossing, with the termination of the street railway, and the station of the Detroit & Bay City and Grand Trunk Railroads. This is a convenient place of arrival and departure, as the Woodward Avenue cars will take you to and from the center of the city.

Three blocks beyond the R. R. crossing, on the southwest corner of Woodward Avenue and the Boulevard, you will notice the brick chapel of the North Baptist Society. At this point you can take the electric cars, and a rapid ride of about six miles will take you within a few hundred feet of the stock farm and widely known Log House of Senator T. W. Palmer, which is well worthy of a visit, and visitors are always welcome. There are many old relics in the house, and the herds of Jersey cows and collection of Percheron horses form an attractive feature, and delightful winding walks and driveways are numerous.

Returning to Woodward Avenue and going over its entire route to the river, you will find the main Ferry landing with boats running frequently to Canada and Belle Isle.

Jefferson Avenue.

This may be called the oldest and most aristocratic thoroughfare in the city, its characteristics are French conservatism, and modern segregation.

By many persons it is deemed not less beautiful than Woodward, and an afternoon can be pleasantly devoted to objects on and near it.

HIGH SCHOOL, AND HEAD OF GRISWOLD STREET.

Taking the cars going east from Woodward Avenue, you proceed up Jefferson Avenue, passing very soon on the right, old Fireman's Hall, now occupied by the Water Commission. The block above is occupied by the Biddle House Hotel. The next street is Brush Street and on the right two blocks away is the depot of the D., G. H. & M. R. R. and the L. S. & M. S. R. R. Soon after the lofty and imposing building of the Academy of the Sacred Heart, in charge of the sisters of that name, is seen; and almost immediately afterwards, on the left, is the Catholic Church of SS. Peter and Paul, the oldest church building in the city.

In the same block is the large and imposing Jesuit College, built of stone and constituting one of the architectural features of the avenue. Almost opposite, on the right at Hastings Street, is the unique building known as the Art Museum, where many exceedingly valuable pictures and Japanese curios are always on exhibition. From this point numbers of fine residences pass rapidly before you; and many of them are very attractive. The handsome stone edifice on the right, with its tower and chime of bells, is Christ's Episcopal Church, and on the left, a little further on, is the Jefferson Avenue Presbyterian Church and Chapel; soon after, on the right, the Gas Works come in sight quite near the avenue. Three blocks further takes you across the bridge extending over the D. & M. R. R. Another three blocks and you will cross the Chene Street car track, leading to the northern part of the city. One block further and you come to Joseph Campau Avenue, and at the foot of this street is the ferry to Walkerville and the boat houses of the Excelsior and Detroit Clubs; the regatta grand stand is usually located near here.

Near the eastern limits of the city, on McDougall Avenue, at the left, is a very large and wide-spreading build-

THE PUBLIC LIBRARY.

ing, the St. Vincent's Catholic Female Orphan Asylum. Soon after, on the right, you pass the Protestant Orphan Asylum. Leaving the cars here, a walk of some five blocks on Elmwood Avenue will bring you to Elmwood Cemetery, where an hour or more can be spent very pleasantly among the many beautiful walks and drives and monuments. Returning towards Jefferson Avenue, you will see on the right the Church and Parochial School of Our Lady of Help, and on the left the Building and grounds of the Michigan Athletic Club.

Again taking Jefferson Avenue to the eastward, within the distance of a block from Elmwood, you pass on the right the immense stove factory and warerooms of the Michigan Stove Company; and immediately afterwards, the stump of the Old Pontiac Tree, like some Rip Van Winkle of the forest, stands before you. The tree was so named from a tradition that it was the silent witness of the battle of Bloody Bridge, where on July 31, 1763, Captain Dalzell and many of his command were surprised and slain during the progress of the Pontiac conspiracy. Two blocks further at the right on Jefferson Avenue, and standing back some distance from the street, you will see the U. S. Marine Hospital with its graceful verandas at each story. Turning in on the left you can visit Mt. Elliott Cemetery. One of the chief points of interest here, is the grave and tombstone of Colonel John Francis Hamtramck, the first American commandant at Detroit. He was originally buried in the graveyard of St. Anne's, but in 1866, the remains were placed in an oaken casket, and deposited in Mount Elliott. The grave is located at the intersection of Shawe and Resurrection Avenues. The inscription on the stone is as follows:

BUILDING OF THE YOUNG MEN'S CHRISTIAN ASSOCIATION.

Sacred
to the Memory of
John Francis Hamtramck, Esq.,
Colonel of the 1st United States Regiment of Infantry
and
Commandant of
Detroit and its Dependencies.
He departed this life on the 11th of April, 1803,
Aged 45 years, 7 months & 28 days.
True Patriotism
And a zealous attachment to National liberty,
joined to a laudable ambition,
led him into Military service at an early
period of his life.
He was a soldier even before he was a man.
He was an active participator
in all the Dangers, Difficulties and honors
of the Revolutionary War;
And his heroism and uniform good conduct
procured him the attention and personal thanks of
the immortal Washington.
The United States in him have lost
A valuable officer and a good citizen,
And Society an Useful and Pleasant Member;
to his family the loss is incalculable,
and his friends will never forget
the Memory of Hamtramck.
This humble monument is placed over
his Remains
by the officers who had the Honor
to serve under his command—
A small but grateful tribute to
his merit
and
his worth.

Opposite the cemetery is the Capuchin Church and Monastery. Another two blocks on Jefferson will bring you to Beaufait Avenue and the depot of the Belt Line Railroad. Five blocks further on you will reach Frontenac Boulevard and the bridge to Belle Isle Park. If the weather is not too warm, by all means walk across, and, midway on the bridge, you will have a beautiful view of the river and of the large variety of steam and sail vessels that continually move through this, the finest strait of fresh water on the globe. The Park itself is mentioned

FIRE ENGINE HOUSE HEAD OF CLIFFORD STREET.

elsewhere. Passing Frontenac Avenue, some four or five streets further on, on the right, and close to the river, is an immense tree, and, near it, the old Hamtramck House, once occupied by Col. Hamtramck.

Something over a mile further will bring you to the massive buildings and immense reservoir of the Water Works, supplying between 30,000,000 and 40,000,000 gallons of water daily. If you make this trip in cherry time, go a mile or two further, and taste the Grosse Pointe cherries, enjoy the beach of the beautiful Lake St. Clair, and see the well-located and handsome Grosse Pointe Casino and the numerous beautiful summer residences, with their spacious and attractive grounds.

On your return towards the city, if you turn to the right at Rivard street and go three blocks north, you will come to Fort street, where you will see on the north side, and four doors from Rivard, the house No. 253, in which Gen. Grant, then Lieutenant, lived during his stay in Detroit, from 1846 to 1851.

Two blocks from Jefferson Avenue, on Congress street, and near St. Antoine street, at No. 185, is the house in which John Brown, "whose soul is marching on," and others, held a preliminary meeting, which resulted in the Harper's Ferry raid.

Returning to Jefferson Avenue, and riding westward a little over a mile, to the termination of the route, you will reach Third Street, and the depot of the Michigan Central Railroad.

From the dock connected with this depot, the cars run on to the railroad ferries, and are transferred across the river.

CENTRAL METHODIST EPISCOPAL CHURCH.

Gratiot Avenue.

An interesting morning trip can be made by the Gratiot Avenue cars, through the German quarter.

Indeed, Gratiot Avenue is a good exponent of the thrift and energy of our German citizens. There is an air of calm and settled content in all that appertains to the locality.

Taking the cars at the Campus Martius, and going through Monroe Avenue, the first street is Farmer Street, and one block to the east is the Police Headquarters, and two blocks further, and also on the east side, at Randolph Street, is the Lyceum Theatre. Ferry's immense seed warehouse occupies one-half of the block. Going on through a portion of Randolph Street and Miami Avenue to Gratiot Avenue, a ride of two blocks will disclose on the right, about a block away, the tall and well-finished building devoted to Municipal Courts, and also the County Jail. One block further, also on the right, you will see St. Mary's Hospital, and also the Detroit College of Medicine.

At Russell Street, one block away, on the left, you will see the graceful spire of St. John's Lutheran Church, the largest and finest Lutheran Church in the city; and also, at Russell Street, on the left, you will notice a Police Station at the corner, and going northerly, on Russell, you pass the hay and wood market on the right, and approach the extensive and outwardly attractive House of Correction. Much time may be profitably spent here in a tour of the buildings, shops and grounds. It is one of the largest and best-managed institutions of its kind in the world, and has an average of 700 inmates, chiefly employed in making chairs.

This is the only city institution that is not only self-supporting but also a source of revenue, and there are probably

ST. JOHN'S EPISCOPAL CHURCH AND RECTORY.

few penal institutions of the kind in the world conducted on so successful a business basis. During its existence it has cared for and maintained about 25,000 prisoners and turned over to the city the enormous sum of $290,000. It has also kept intact the city's investment of about $200,-000, and has added to it, over and above the cash turned over, at least $200,000 additional, thus showing a net gain to the city, over and above expenses, of about $500,000.

From the House of Correction you can easily see the old reservoir of the Water Works, which is only about three blocks away. The large brick building about two blocks north of the reservoir in the center of a large square, is the "Little Sisters' Home for the Aged Poor," and nearly a mile away in the same direction, you can see the Polish Cathedral, the largest church in the city, and near it their theological school, and also a convent.

A ride of about six miles on the Gratiot road will bring you to the Grotto of the Blessed Virgin Mary. This is one of the most attractive, and most peculiar, structures connected with church life in the country, and was erected "in memory of the apparition at Lourdes." It is near the Church of the Assumption, and was built through the exertions of Rev. Father A. Vandendriessche, who has been in charge of the parish since 1851. The grotto is located at the end of an avenue of trees nearly 1,000 feet long, planted through the same zeal that caused the grotto to be reared. The entire cost of the structure is estimated at $6,000, though much of the work has been gratuitously performed. It was begun by the blessing of the ground, on the last Sunday of May, 1881, and just a year from that time mass was said for the first time.

Within the grotto, ten feet of the walls on either hand are occupied by four rows of massive stones, all dressed to the square, the face of each stone bearing an emblem of

WOODWARD AVENUE BAPTIST CHURCH.

the church or of the Virgin. They are also inscribed with the names of various deceased priests.

On each of the stones in the ceiling will be engraved the name of one of the popes, with the date of his death, and the name of the donor of the stone. At the base of the arch is a narrow projection or cornice of stone, bearing on its sides the inscriptions: "Hail, Mary, full of grace; the Lord is with thee;" "Holy Mary, mother of God, pray for us sinners," the words being separated by stars. On the rear cornice is the word "sanctus" thrice repeated. The floor will be of marble.

Grand River Avenue.

This avenue is justly characterized as broad, slow, English and self-satisfied. It has a large future before it, but develops more slowly than any other of the older avenues leading into the country. Although not possessed of any specially attractive buildings it is well worthy of attention. Three blocks from Woodward avenue on the right is the Industrial School, one of the oldest and most deserving of the charities of the city.

A ride of a few blocks brings you to the Cass School and the Second Avenue Presbyterian Church, and soon after, on the left, the Simpson M. E. Church. Three blocks more brings you to the crossing of Trumbull and Lincoln avenues, with their numerous and substantial residences. The church on the right is the Trumbull Avenue Presbyterian, and that on the left on Myrtle street is Epiphany Reformed Episcopal Church.

At Nineteenth street is the D. & B. C. R. R. station, and here the street cars stop. Just across the track is the extensive factory of the National Pin Company. A mile beyond is the 300 acre seed farm of D. M. Ferry & Co.,

UNITARIAN CHURCH.

and almost all the year round you may see scores of "weeders" and "pickers" at work in these broad fields.

Michigan Avenue.

This busy, bartering, Celtic, and Jewish avenue is one of the greatest thoroughfares in the city. Nothing of special note is to be seen until at Trumbull avenue, on the left, is St. Peter's Episcopal Church, and also a police station.

At Thirteenth street, on the right, is St. Boniface Catholic Church. Soon after, some two blocks away, on the left, you will see the Tappan School and the Catholic Church and school of St. Vincent de Paul.

At Seventeenth street, on the right, is Immanuel Lutheran Church. Also, on the left, a few blocks away, the cattle yards, the Car Wheel Works and the Bridge and Iron Works. Soon after the street car line brings you to the Junction, where the trains of the M. C. R. R., the L. S. & M. S. and G. T. R. R. transfer passengers or baggage. Near here is located the largest car manufactory in the United States, the shops of the M. C. R. R., and several extensive brick yards.

Griswold Street.

This is the "Wall Street" of Detroit, and hence will claim a visit. Banks, insurance and real estate offices and lawyers occupy both sides of the street for several blocks.

The Postoffice and Custom House is on the northwest corner of Griswold and Larned, and the Western Union Telegraph office on the southeast corner of Griswold and Congress.

Half a block west of Griswold, on Congress, is the office of the Evening Journal, and one block west of Griswold,

FIRST PRESBYTERIAN CHURCH.

on Larned, are the offices of the Free Press and Evening News.

Two blocks from Griswold, on Larned, is the headquarters of the Fire Commission. Two of the steamers are kept here, and half an hour or more can be spent very enjoyably in an inspection of the apparatus. To see the well trained horses jump to their places when the gong sounds is alone worth the time bestowed. Near State street, on the east side of Griswold, is Whitney's Opera House.

West Fort and River Streets.

No tour of the city would be complete that did not include a trip down West Fort Street. If you start from Woodward Avenue, you will soon pass the site of the new postoffice on the right at Shelby Street. Old Fort Shelby formerly occupied the ground in this locality.

At the corner of Second Street, on the right, is Grace Episcopal Church, built of Milwaukee brick. A block further on, at the left is the superbly beautiful stone church of the Fort Street Presbyterian Society. The several blocks on the left beyond Third Street include the site of the new Union depot. The large brick building on the right between Fourth and Fifth streets is the Sanitarium.

On and on you go, crossing the bridge over the M. C. R. R. near Eleventh street and at Twelfth street on the river are the grounds of the Union Depot Co., where all trains on the Wabash & St. Louis, Canadian Pacific, Flint & Pere Marquette and Detroit, Lansing & Northern Railroads arrive and depart. At Eighteenth street, you will see on the right, the large and imposing convent of the Good Shepherd; the two steeples just east of this point are those of St. Anne's Roman Catholic Church.

HARPER HOSPITAL.

About eight blocks further, on the left, are large tobacco factories and warehouses, and on the right a little further, at Clark avenue is the Riverside Mineral Springs and bathing establishment.

Two blocks beyond Clark avenue on Fort street are the spacious grounds and attractive buildings of St. Luke's Hospital, and about two miles further, the large and attractive grounds of Woodmere Cemetery.

Turning on Clark avenue toward the river, you take the River road, and still in the car, keep on to Fort Wayne, a first-class fortification costing nearly half a million dollars. Here are cannons and soldiers in abundance. The fort proper, within which are the barracks, lies to the east of the officers' quarters, and is reached by a foot bridge crossing over the moat; the magazine is also located within the fort. Visitors are welcome to visit any part of the fort or grounds except the casemates, which are locked; and you will not be allowed to walk on the parapet slopes. The houses on the east side of the fort are occupied by the married men and their families. On the parade ground, which lies between the officers' quarters and the river, stands a saluting battery of light 12-pounders, and a little to the left is the morning and evening gun, which is fired every morning and also at the sunset hour. The grounds embrace sixty-five acres.

A short distance beyond the Fort are the extensive grounds of the Detroit International Exposition, and its numerous and enormous buildings will easily attract the eye. Several hundred thousand dollars have been expended in this enterprise, and it is the most extensive and beautifully located local exposition ever provided. It was first opened September 17, 1889.

GRACE HOSPITAL.

A Carriage Drive.

The following route will bring before you some of the most desirable portions of the city. Up Michigan Avenue to Washington, around Grand Circus Parks on Adams Avenue to Cass Avenue, up Cass to Alexandrine Avenue, west on Alexandrine to Second Street, down Second, around Cass Park, still on Second to Lafayette Avenue, west on Lafayette to Trumbull Avenue, up Trumbull to Grand River Avenue, along Grand River to Twelfth Street, up Twelfth to the Boulevard and east and south along it to the Bridge and across to Belle Isle Park.

Belle Isle Park.

This Park contains 700 acres and was purchased in 1879 at a cost of $200,000, and over $400,000 additional has been expended upon it. An elegant Casino, boat-houses, and other needful buildings have been erected, canals excavated and the low marsh lands along the edge of the island are being transformed into water and driveways.

The underbrush has also been largely removed, rustic bridges erected and a variety of attractions and conveniences provided. The walks and drives are pleasing, and the Park carriages for a nominal sum will take you all over the island. The boating facilities in the canals are exceptional and from any point there are attractive views.

The passing vessels afford a continually changing scene, and altogether the view on a summer day is hardly equalled elsewhere.

There is an abundance of trees of native growth, and in the season no more attractive and delightful park can be found in this or any other land, and eventually it is possibly destined to surpass all other resorts of like nature.

During 1889 a bridge was completed from the foot of

IRVING SCHOOL.

the Boulevard to the island at a cost of $300,000. It was opened to the public on May 12 of that year, is provided with a draw, and is a little over 2,000 feet long. Travelers on foot or in carriages are amply provided for, and one of the most pleasing views in or near the city is the view up and down the river from the center of the bridge.

The Boulevard, which at a distance of about three miles from the center surrounds the city on three sides, bears an important relation to the Park as well as to the city. Its inception dates from 1879, and although not fully opened, the near future will see it completed, and for all time it must prove one of the most attractive driveways in or near the city. It is from one hundred and fifty to two hundred feet wide, and will be about twelve miles long.

Historical Sketch of Detroit.

Scarcely twenty decades have passed since the founding of Detroit. During nearly all of these years, and up to a very recent period, the prosperity of the city was greatly hindered by the ease-loving and extremely careful spirit of its earliest founders, and their cautious descendants.

It was this spirit and education that provided the early streets of only twelve or twenty feet in width, and that resisted the extension of the city, through the opening of roads and streets across the narrow farms that on either side hemmed in the town.

This same spirit in later owners still "seeks its own," but, fortunately, it has no longer power to hinder the city's growth and gain.

In 1805, nearly ten decades of years after the founding of the city, its swaddling bands were loosened by the fire that swept away, not only houses and stores, but streets as well. This most fortunate event, which is happily commemorated in the emblematic seal of the city, with its mottos of *Resurget Cineribus*, "she rises from the ashes," and *Speramus Meliora*, "we hope for better times," gave us an entirely new plan for the city, with streets and avenues and a Campus Martius and Grand Circus that will be an honor to the city, and a joy and delight for a thousand years and more.

The French *habitans* protested vociferously and vigorously against the innovations of the newer plan, declaring that the lots above the present City Hall would "never be built upon, and were only fit for pasturage." Fortunately their protest was of no avail. Twenty years later, in 1826, another great advance was gained, the grounds included in

THE

IS ONE OF THE MOST

POPULAR INSTITUTIONS,

AND THE

POPULATION OF WAYNE COUNTY

HAS BEEN AS FOLLOWS:

1820,	3,574
1830,	6,781
1840,	24,173
1850,	42,756
1860,	75,547
1870,	119,068
1880,	166,444
1890,	256,838

THE THOMPSON HOME FOR OLD LADIES.

MEMORANDA

TO BE

MEMORIZED

A deposit in bank
Gives standing and rank.

Waste & Want are
Still in partnership.

A

BANK
OO

OFTEN LEADS TO

A

BRICK
LOC

He who has silver ahead
Will not fear silver hairs.

Wayne **C**ounty **S**avings **B**ank.
Well **C**onsidered **S**afe **B**estowed.

HOME OF THE FRIENDLESS.

Fort Shelby, with the surrounding military reserve, were then relinquished by the United States to the Corporation. The lands covered nearly twelve blocks in the very center of the city, and the reservation had been a formidable obstacle to growth and improvement. The Fort proper lay between what is now Fort and Lafayette, Griswold and Wayne Streets.

The grading down of the Fort embankment, the filling in at the same time of the low lands along the river, the opening of numerous new streets, and the platting and exposing to sale by the city, at nominal prices, of hundreds of the newly acquired lots platted from the old Fort grounds, marked a distinct era in the city's life, and afforded the largest inducement that had been offered for new citizens.

During the next decade the population increased over four hundred per cent, the emigration from the Eastern and New England States was unprecedented, and amounted almost to a mania; fleets of steamboats that outnumbered those now arriving brought thousands of new comers to Detroit and the West, and helped to relieve the town from French control, and during the same period the boundary of the city was pushed outward on both its eastern and western sides.

During the decades from 1840 to 1860, communication was opened with the interior, through various plank roads, several railroads were pushed clear across the State, and others connected with railroads from the East, giving a great impetus to the city's growth. During this same period, the territory included within the city was again doubled by additions on the east and west.

The years between 1860 and 1870, covering the period of the war with the South, brought great prosperity to Detroit. Immense amounts of new capital was created and invested in the city, the suburbs were first made accessible through the street railways, the architectural ornamenta-

ROMAN CATHOLIC CHURCH OF SS. PETER AND PAUL.

tion of both stores and houses greatly increased, and the manufacturing interests of the city grew apace.

Meantime nearly all the older holders of the larger farms within the city, and without in immediate proximity, passed away, and as the property has been largely sold and divided, the octopus of conservatism that so long held the city in its grasp, has released its hold, and the city has started forward for a larger place in the front rank with leading cities of the continent.

It is a fact capable of a demonstration, that the West has been so largely explored and examined, and the railroad routes and sites of cities so fully determined, that no other new large city will be located either in the West or East.

The cities already well established with favorable locations and facilities will largely gather to themselves the growth of the future, and all such cities will increase in wealth and population much faster than in former years.

Detroit, with its exceptional opportunities and advantages, is certain to obtain its full share of the gain resulting from the conditions named, and as a manufacturing and residence city it will inevitably take a still more advanced position.

In the way of elegant business and commercial structure the city has gained more in the last twenty years than in all its past before that time, and the same is true with regard to the adornment it now enjoys through its hundreds upon hundreds of elegant residences, more in number proportionate to the population than is possessed by any other city in America, and when the attractive surroundings are considered, more than are to be found in Philadelphia or New York.

The growth in population from time to time is indicated in the following :

THE ART MUSEUM.

Years.	Population.	Years.	Population.
1796,	500	1850,	21,019
1810,	770	1854,	40,127
1812,	800	1860,	45,619
1817,	900	1864,	53,170
1819,	1,110	1868,	68,827
1800,	1,442	1870,	79.577
1828,	1,517	1874,	101,225
1830,	2,222	1880.	116,342
1834,	4,968	1884,	134,834
1840.	9,192	1890.	205,876
1845,	13,065		

The number of families in 1890 was 42,150, and there were 65,120 children between the ages of five and twenty years.

The municipal statistics all indicate an unusually well managed city government. The Fire Department numbers a force of 261, with 17 steamers, 6 hook and ladder companies, three chemical engines and upwards of 250 fire alarm boxes. The police force includes 371 persons, with 11 buildings and nearly 200 signal boxes.

The Public School buildings number 52, with sittings for 25,000 children. The letter carriers number over 100. The valuation of personal property in 1891 was $39,423,070, of real estate, $136,026,640, a total of $175,450,310.

With all its other advantages the city is behind no others in the number of its churches and charitable institutions. For more than two decades an average of five new churches have been built each year, and in the various charitable and philanthropic institutions over 1,000,000 dollars are invested.

The increasingly appreciated favorable location of the city as a place of summer resort, because of its water communications and its exceptional health record, together with its wide reputation as a beautiful residence city, is yearly attracting from the interior of Michigan, and also

CHRIST EPISCOPAL CHURCH.

from the far East, scores of persons who come here to enjoy the wealth they have secured elsewhere.

Here we have no fear of a flood or of an overflow, we seldom experience the extremes of heat or cold, and a larger proportion of citizens live "under their own vine and fig tree" than in any other city of the size of Detroit.

The increase of wealth and leisure in the city is indicated very clearly in the increased attention paid to athletic sports and in the large amounts expended for buildings and appliances by the several athletic clubs.

The greater demand for such instrumentalities arises not only from the natural increase in the population, but because young men especially are attracted to the cities, and in a given number of people a much larger number of young men will be found in a city than in a country district.

A leading and influential factor in the proper development of these desirable societies exists in the thoroughly equipped and efficiently officered gymnasium of the Young Men's Christian Association. This organization was the first to procure the latest and best gymnastic appliances.

It is also true that other highly creditable athletic organizations exist. Of these the Detroit Athletic Club is the oldest. Its building, located on the west side of Woodward Avenue, just above Canfield avenue, with its appurtenances, cost $30,000.

A newer but none the less popular and valuable organization, the Michigan Athletic Club, has its building on the corner of Congress Street and Elmwood Avenue, where it owns fully a block of land, its entire property representing a value of $65,000, the building and apparatus costing $31,000.

The opportunities for recreation at Detroit are not confined to those on land. Within easy reach of the city, at the upper end of Lake St. Clair, there is one of the most

JEFFERSON AVENUE RAILROAD BRIDGE.

noted of hunting and fishing grounds. The marshy waters in the season are the feeding places of myriads of ducks, and the waters are equally thronged with fish of many desirable kinds. The rare opportunities here offered have caused the establishment of several fishing and shooting clubs and a number of extensive club houses have been located along the lake and on the higher grounds, and several individuals have erected fishing cottages and to the profit of their health spend days together in semi-isolation from the cares of life. The most prominent clubs making use of the facilities here afforded are the Lake St. Clair Fishing and Shooting Club, the North Channel Shooting Club, the Detroit Hunting and Fishing Association, and the Michigan Gun Club.

Although possessing exceptional facilities for boating, there has been little popular enthusiasm for this sport for some years past. The American people as a whole seldom think about or engage in more than one thing at a time, and of late our mind has been on land sports instead of those upon the water, but in due time the pendulum of fashion will again swing over the water, and boat clubs will be "all the go" and "on the go" on one of the finest stretches of water to be found in all the world.

A most interesting increase in the attention paid to art has been developed since 1870, and a large share of the growth may be properly traced to the Art Loan Exhibition held in 1883.

The principal ocular outgrowth of that exhibition is the building of the Detroit Museum of Art, located on the corner of Jefferson Avenue and Hastings Street. The lot, costing $25,000, was donated by citizens interested in art, and a fund of $100,000 for the building was raised by popular subscription. An Art Academy has been established, a number of classes for the study of various branches of art and courses of lectures provided, and an

VIEWS IN ELMWOOD CEMETERY.

excellent equipment exists in a large number of valuable paintings and models belonging to the Museum.

That there is marked interest in musical matters is evident to any one who pays any heed to what may be seen daily and almost hourly on any street. You can scarce enter a street car without encountering one or more lads or misses with music roll or violin case. The rising generation is paying vastly more attention to music than was paid two decades ago, or even ten years ago.

Several thoroughly equipped schools or conservatories, with from one to a number of hundreds of pupils, have grown up, and these, with a large corps of teachers, are doing excellent work in giving instruction in both vocal and instrumental music.

General statistics as to the amount and value of manufactured products in almost any period, or gathered through any instrumentality, are of comparatively little value. If a firm or corporation have special advantages that some one would perhaps copy if attention was called to them, their success is not likely to be noised abroad. Many manufacturing institutions owe their prosperity to the "still hunt" method of calling attention to their wares rather than to the amount of business that they are doing. If it becomes apparent that any person is doing much better than the average, there are a hundred persons who wish to obtain a share of the profits by engaging in the same business. For these reasons the figures obtained are often incomplete, inaccurate or misleading.

If, on the contrary, the business of a firm or corporation is not remunerative, there is a natural temptation to increase the credit or business standing by overestimates or the giving of prospective conditions rather than present facts. All estimates, therefore, of this nature are liable to be either overestimated or underestimated, and are of necessity followed by an interrogation point; if this mark is not

THE PONTIAC TREE.

always printed its exists in the mind of those who look beneath the words or figures and is supplied as needed.

Some facts, however, are patent even to a casual observer. When the eye sees large and wide-spreading factories where it is known that formerly no building existed, observes volumes of smoke pouring from numerous chimneys, hears the hum and hammer of machinery, and from time to time notices hundreds of workers going in or coming out of a building, it is ocularly and aurally demonstrated that a large amount of work is being performed. If further demonstration is desired, the loaded trucks or cars that leave the premises will often supply the evidence.

Judged by these positive standards the general prosperity of an establishment may be fairly predicated, and there are many such in Detroit. There are twenty-one banks, and they have all told about $10,000,000 of capital.

The Board of Trade.

This is located on the southeast corner of Jefferson Avenue and Griswold Street.

The members of the board protect each other by agreeing upon a uniform scale of fees or commissions for buying or selling grain and produce. In the delivering of grain, the transfer of a receipt from one of the railroad elevators, specifying that the grain is in store and giving the number of bushels, is accepted as an actual delivery. From February 25, 1879, an initiation fee of $250 was required from all new members, and on March 4, 1882, it was voted to raise the fee to $500 as soon as one hundred members were obtained.

There are now about one hundred members. Persons seeking admission as members must be of legal age, residents of the city or having a permanent business therein, or

Mark these Remarkable Facts and Figures

The Amounts on Deposit January 1st Each Year

IN THE

Wayne County Savings Bank

HAVE BEEN AS FOLLOWS:

1872,	$ 120,987 51	1882,	$3,127,362 76
1873,	612,079 72	1883,	3,399,309 86
1874,	694,944 58	1884,	3,567,412 34
1875,	1,114,186 90	1885,	3,282,937 17
1876,	1,327,206 71	1886,	3,682,272 99
1877,	1,556,862 57	1887,	3,774,447 00
1878,	1,367,138 12	1888,	3,942,559 33
1879,	1,466,881 55	1889,	4,311,178 90
1880,	1,752,091 49	1890,	4,680,817 53
1881,	2,395,014 49	1891,	5,036,963 06

NOT A DEPOSITOR.

The population of Detroit in 1874 was 101,225 and the deposits in the Wayne County Bank on January 1st of that year showed an average of $7 for every person.

The population in 1880 was 116,342, and the deposits on January 1st of that year showed an average of over $15 for each person.

The population in 1890 was 205,876, and the deposits on January 1st of that year showed an average of over $22 for each person in Detroit.

Comparing the population of the City with the number of depositors in 1874 one person in every 33 was a depositor in this bank, in 1880 one person in every 16, and in 1890 one person in every 20.

It is a well known fact that depositors in savings banks are the most steadfast of clients or customers, and keeping this fact in view, the advantages resulting to depositors are clearly shown in the fact that the average amount to the credit of each depositor in the Wayne County Savings Bank in 1874 was $222, in 1880, $252, and in 1890, $458.

be members of a similar commercial organization in some other city. Their application must be indorsed by two members of the board, and after five days' notice, seven affirmative votes by the directors will elect them to membership. The business acts of every member are subject to investigation by the Board of Directors, if called in question by any other member.

The annual meeting is held on the first Tuesday in March, and the term of office begins on the Tuesday following. A president, first and second vice-presidents, and eight directors are elected yearly, who control the affairs of the organization, appoint the secretary, treasurer, and inspectors, and hold regular meetings on the second Tuesday of each month. At each annual meeting they report the amount to be assessed upon each member the succeeding year. The revenue of the board is derived principally from the inspection of grain, at twenty-five cents per car load, and from dues of members.

City Taxes; When and How Payable.

The estimates of taxes, as submitted by the Controller, are required to be adopted by the Common Council before April 5 of each year, and must be submitted to the Board of Estimates in time to be confirmed by the Council before April 15. While the members of the Council are considering the estimates, the Board of Assessors have been completing their valuation of the property to be taxed; and, at least two weeks before April 1, they are required to give notice that they will sit until April 5 to hear complaints and make corrections in the valuations. After this has been done, on or before the third Tuesday of April, they send the completed tax roll to the Board of Aldermen, and within a week thereafter the board of Aldermen begin

UNITED STATES MARINE HOSPITAL.

to hold sessions as a Board of Review to hear complaints, and, if necessary, to correct the rolls. Their sessions continue not over sixteen days, after which, about the middle of May, the rolls are confirmed. The assessors then compute the amount of taxes payable on each valuation contained on the rolls, and taxes may be paid during the month of July without percentage. Since the law of 1879, if the clerks in office are so busy that they cannot receive all taxes offered, lists of property, with names of owners, may be handed in on or before July 25, and the parties can have until August 10 to pay the amounts, if there is no opportunity of paying sooner. On the first of August, interest, at the rate of one per cent. a month, is added for July, and at the same rate the first of each month until the first of January, unless the tax is paid. If not paid by the first of January, the six per cent. that has accrued is added to the original tax, and interest is charged at the rate of ten per cent. per annum until the tax is paid. If not paid by the first of February, the Receiver of Taxes is authorized to advertise the property for sale; but as it takes some time to prepare them, the lists are usually not printed until about May 1, when the property is advertised for sale for four successive weeks. After this the cost of advertising, amounting to about fifty cents, is added, and interest continues to be reckoned at the rate of ten per cent. per annum. If the tax is not paid the property is sold about June 1, the exact day being discretionary with the Receiver of Taxes. The sale indicates only that the purchaser is entitled to the use of the property purchased for the number of years agreed upon at time of sale; but if the owner neglects to redeem it, the sale is confirmed by a regular transfer of the title by the city. Records of sales are filed in the City Treasurer's office. The property can be redeemed at any time within one year after sale, by paying the amount due at the time of sale and interest at the

ENTRANCE TO MOUNT ELLIOTT CEMETERY.

rate of ten per cent. per annum. Soon after the sale a list of all property on which the taxes have not been paid, nor cancelled by sales, is furnished by the Receiver to the City Treasurer, to be thereafter collected through him.

At the annual sale, unless some private person bids the amount of the tax, all lands on which taxes are unpaid are sold to the city, and the amounts received for back taxes in the Treasurer's office are credited as receipts from "City Bids."

Taxes or assessments for the building of sidewalks and sewers, or for paving of streets, are kept entirely distinct from the regular city taxes, and are payable within thirty days from the time the rolls are placed in hands of Receiver. If not paid paid within thirty days, the Receiver of Taxes can, at his discretion, advertise for sale the property on which these taxes are levied.

State and County Taxes: When Payable.

Under the tax law of March 14, 1882, and Act of June 6, 1883, the State and County taxes for each current year become a lien on the property on December 1, and one per cent. on the amount, is allowed the township treasurers for collecting the same. After January 1 four per cent. is allowed the township treasurers. Within the city of Detroit the taxes are payable to the county treasurer up to December 16 without any percentage. If not paid by December 16, four per cent. is added to the amount of the original tax, which must be paid by the first of February, unless the time is extended by the Common Council or the Township Board; but not over one month of additional time can be granted. If not paid by the first of March, two per cent. additional is added, and then one per cent.

a month up to June 1, and if not then paid, a further sum of twenty per cent. per year is charged until paid.

On the first of March a list of all lands on which the taxes are unpaid is forwarded by the county treasurer to the auditor-general, and if the taxes remain unpaid one year or more after the first of July, the lands are then sold on the first of May in the next year. The sale is made by the county treasurer, who, within twenty days after the sale, must file with the clerk of the Circuit Court a list of the lands sold, and unless objection is made, within eight days thereafter the sale is confirmed. At any time within one year thereafter the court can set aside the sale, upon such terms as are deemed just; but no sale can be set aside after the purchaser or his assignee has been in possession for five years.

House and Store Numbers.

The regulations provide one number for every twenty feet, the numbers alternating from one side of the street to the other. On all streets running nearly north and south, or at right angles to the river and parallel with Woodward Avenue, the numbers begin at the south end of the street, or the end nearest the river, and number towards the city limits; and when the streets do not extend through to the river, the numbers begin at their southerly end, near some one of the principal avenues,—Jefferson, Michigan, Grand River, or Gratiot. Going from the river, the odd numbers, as 1, 3, 5, and 7, are on the left hand, and the even numbers, as 2, 4, 6, and 8, on the right hand side of the street. On all streets east of Woodward Avenue, and running nearly east and west, or at right angles with Woodward Avenue and parallel with the river, the numbers begin at Woodward Avenue, or the end nearest to it, and

GROSSE POINTE.

number outwards towards the city limits, the odd numbers on the north or left hand side going from Woodward Avenue, and the even numbers on the south side of the street. On all streets west of Woodward Avenue, and running nearly east and west or at right angles with Woodward Avenue and parallel with the river, the numbers begin at Woodward Avenue, or the end nearest it, and number outwards towards the city limits; the odd numbers being on the south or left-hand side of the street, and the even numbers on the north side of the street. The only exception to this rule is in the case of Jefferson Avenue, where the numbers begin at Second Street and run east, the odd numbers being on the north side of the street, and on Madison Avenue, where the even numbers are on the south side. There is an average of about forty numbers to a block, including those on both sides of the street.

Street Railroads.

The routes of the several lines are as follows: Jefferson Avenue—from Third up Jefferson Avenue to City Water Works.

The Woodward Avenue Line extends from Brush on Atwater to Woodward Avenue and up this avenue to the railroad crossing.

The Cass Avenue and Third Street Line extends from Jefferson Avenue up Third to Larned, on Larned to Griswold, up Griswold to State, around State to Cass Avenue, up Cass to Ledyard, on Ledyard to Third, up Third to the Holden Road, and along the Holden Road to the railroad crossing. Cars also run from the Michigan Central Depot up Third to Grand River, and transfer passengers to either the Grand River, Myrtle or Crawford Street Lines.

GEN. GRANT'S OLD HOME.
253 Fort St. East.

The Michigan Avenue Line is operated from Jefferson Avenue up Woodward Avenue to Michigan Avenue, and on Michigan Avenue to the Grand Trunk Junction.

The Gratiot Avenue Line extends from Jefferson Avenue up Woodward Avenue to Monroe Avenue, on Monroe Avenue to Randolph, on Randolph to Gratiot Avenue, and up Gratiot Avenue to Mt. Elliott Avenue.

Some cars, designated as Cross Town cars, go over the entire route of Gratiot and Michigan Avenue Lines for a single fare.

The Chene Street Cars run from foot of Woodward up to Monroe Avenue, and thence through Randolph to Gratiot, and up Gratiot to Chene Street, and north on Chene to the Boulevard. A line from Gratiot south on Chene to Atwater, and east on Atwater to Joseph Campau is operated part of the time.

The Crawford Street Line runs from Grand River north on Crawford to the railroad crossing.

The Congress and Baker Street Line runs from Atwater up Randolph to Congress, on Congress to Seventh, up Seventh to Baker, and on Baker to Twenty-fourth Street, and every other car goes through Twenty-fourth street to Dix Avenue, and on Dix Avenue to the railroad crossing.

The Brush Street Line runs on the Gratiot Avenue route to Brush, up Brush to Ohio, along Ohio to St. Antoine, up St. Antoine to Farnsworth, along Farnsworth to Russell, up Russell to Ferry Avenue, along Ferry to Dequindre. Some cars run on Russell from Ferry Avenue to the railroad crossing.

The Trumbull Avenue Line runs on Michigan Avenue to Trumbull Avenue, and on Trumbull to the railroad crossing.

The East Fort Street Line runs from Woodward Avenue east on Congress to Mt. Elliott Avenue, north on Mt.

THE JOHN BROWN HOUSE,
185 Congress St. East.

Elliott to Fort, and west on Fort to Brush, on Brush to Congress, and thence to Woodward Avenue.

Cars also run from Woodward Avenue through Congress, and on Mt. Elliott to Jefferson Avenue, and on Jefferson Avenue to the Belle Isle Bridge.

The Fort Street and Elmwood Line extends from Woodmere Cemetery southeast along the Dearborn Road to the River Road, thence along the River Road to Clark Avenue, up Clark Avenue to Fort, on Fort to Woodward Avenue, across Woodward and through Cadillac Square to Bates, up Bates to Champlain, through Champlain to Helen, and south on Helen to Jefferson Avenue. Returning, cars come back on same route to Elmwood Avenue, and then go north on Elmwood to Monroe, and on Monroe to Randolph, and along Randolph to Cadillac Square, and from there cross Woodward Avenue to Fort.

The Highland Park Railway Company operate an electric railway, three miles long, on Woodward Avenue, commencing just beyond the railroad crossing. The fare is five cents, and, by arrangement with the city railway, eight cents will pay the fare on both the electric and the Woodward Avenue Lines.

The East Detroit and Grosse Point Railway runs from Gratiot Avenue on Mack Avenue to Baldwin Avenue.

The Myrtle Street Line runs from Twenty-fourth Street through Myrtle Street to Grand River Avenue, and then en route of Grand River Avenue Railway to Jefferson Avenue.

The Grand River Avenue Line runs from Jefferson Avenue, up Woodward Avenue to Grand River Avenue, and on Grand River Avenue to Boulevard.

MICHIGAN CENTRAL RAILROAD DEPOT.

Belt Line Railroad.

This Line extends all around the outskirts of the city, from the M. C. R. R. depot to the junction of Jefferson and Beaufait Avenues. Trains run at frequent and regular intervals and stop at the following places:

Twentieth Street, Bay City Junction, Michigan Avenue, Vinewood Avenue, Twenty-seventh Street, Twenty-fourth Street, Grand River Avenue, Twelfth Street, Holden Road, Woodward Avenue, Peninsular Switch, Milwaukee Avenue and Hastings Street, Russell Street, Milwaukee Junction, Belt Line Junction, Chene Street, Harper Avenue, Boulevard, Gratiot Avenue, Mack Road, Waterloo Street, Champlain Street, Beaufait Station.

The fare is ten cents; twenty-ride tickets one dollar; five-ride tickets twenty-five cents.

The Ferries.

Ferries run from the foot of Woodward Avenue to Belle Isle and also to Windsor every fifteen minutes, and from the foot of Joseph Campau Avenue to Belle Isle and also to Walkerville every thirty minutes.

Steamboat Lines.

There are passenger lines to various points as follows:

From Dock foot of Randolph Street to Chatham and New Baltimore.

From Dock foot of Griswold Street to Club Houses, Star Island, Grande Pointe, Algonac, Marine City, The Oakland, St. Clair, Sarnia, Port Huron and intermediate ports.

From Dock between Griswold and Shelby Streets, east

RAILROAD FERRY DOCK.

to Cleveland, Erie and Buffalo, north to Port Huron, Sault Ste. Marie, Marquette, Houghton, Hancock, Portage Lake, Ashland, Washburn, Bayfield and Duluth.

From Dock foot of Shelby Street to Port Huron.

From Dock foot of First Street east to Cleveland, and north to Port Huron, Sand Beach, Oscoda, Harrisville, Alpena, Rogers City, Cheboygan, Mackinaw and St. Ignace. Also to Put-in-Bay, Kelly's Islands and Sandusky. Also to Ecorce, Wyandotte, Grosse Isle, Trenton, Amherstburg and Sugar Island.

Rates of Hack Fare.

Authorized by City Ordinance.

The drivers or owners of public conveyances may demand and receive for conveying passengers the following rates or prices of fare, and no more, to wit:

For carrying a passenger from one place to another, within the limits of said city, fifty cents. Children, under ten years of age, not exceeding two in number, when accompanied by parents or guardians, shall be carried free of charge. Those in excess of that number shall each be charged half fare.

For the use of any public conveyance by the hour, for not more than four persons, and with the privilege of going from place to place, and stopping as often as required, one dollar and fifty cents per hour for the first hour, and one dollar for each additional hour; and for fractional hours at the rate of one dollar per hour; and for each additional passenger twenty-five cents per hour. For the use by the day of such conveyance, five dollars. For each trunk, fifteen cents; but no charge shall be made for any bag, valise or bundle weighing less than fifty pounds.

POLICE HEAD-QUARTERS.

American District Telegraph Company.

MESSENGER SERVICE.

This Company furnishes reliable boys for errands or service of any sort at twenty-five cents an hour. The office is on Griswold Street between Jefferson Avenue and Larned Street.

Express Offices.

Both the American and United States Express Offices are located on the east side of Woodward Avenue between Larned and Congress Streets. The National Express Company is at No. 6 Monroe Avenue.

Telegraph Offices.

Telegraph offices are located on the southeast corner of Griswold and Congress Streets and on the west side of Griswold Street near Jefferson Avenue.

Railroad Depots.

Michigan Central, Detroit, Lansing & Northern and Flint & Pere Marquette Railroads, foot of Third Street. Detroit, Grand Haven & Milwaukee, Grand Trunk and Lake Shore & Michigan Southern, foot of Brush Street.

Wabash & St. Louis Railroad, foot of Twelfth Street.

Hotels.

The four leading hotels are the Russell House, facing the Campus Martius, the Cadillac on Michigan Avenue between Rowland Street and Washington Avenue, the

MUNICIPAL COURT BUILDING.

Wayne opposite the Michigan Central Railroad depot and the Normandie on Congress Street just east of Woodward Avenue.

Lunch Rooms.

The leading lunch rooms, that are entirely free from liquor serving, are Crawford's Dairy Lunch, on east side of Woodward Avenue, between Congress and Larned Streets, the Women's Exchange rooms in the Y. M. C. A. building, corner of Grand River and Griswold, and the Delicatessen, on Gratiot Avenue, half a block from Woodward Avenue.

Opera Houses and Public Halls.

Whitney's Opera House, Griswold near State Street.
Detroit Opera House, facing Campus Martius.
Lyceum Theatre, Randolph Street, between Monroe Avenue and Champlain Street.
Philharmonic Hall, corner Lafayette Avenue and Shelby Street.
Detroit Rink, Larned Street between Bates and Randolph Streets.
Merrill Hall, corner of Jefferson and Woodward Avenues.
Princess Rink, Second Avenue, corner of High Street.
Y. M. C. A. Building, corner of Grand River and Griswold Streets.
Art Museum, corner Jefferson avenue and Rivard Street.

The River and Islands.

London has its Thames, Paris the Seine, Rome the Tiber, and New York the Hudson; but in everything the Detroit river excels them all, and is undoubtedly one of the most

ST. MARY'S HOSPITAL.

remarkable in the world. It forms a natural boundary between the United States and Upper Canada, separating the State of Michigan from the Province of Ontario; the boundary line opposite Detroit is about midway of the stream, and for most of the distance nearest the Canadian shore. The United States thus has jurisdiction over the larger portion. The greatest width of the river is three miles; in its narrowest point, opposite the city, it is a little over half a mile wide. Its average width is one mile. The depth varies from ten to sixty feet, with an average of thirty-four feet. The river bottom, for the most part, is sandy or stony. It is navigable for vessels of the largest class, is almost entirely free from obstructions of any sort, and offers one of the largest and safest harbors in the world. London is the largest port, but more tonnage passes Detroit than ever enters the Thames. There are but few streams in the world that rival the Detroit in purity and in amount of water discharged. The incline amounts to one and one-half inches per mile, or three feet for its entire length. The elevation above sea level, at a point opposite the Marine Hospital, is five hundred and seventy-seven feet. The river is not generally frozen over until the latter part of December or January, but in extreme cold weather the ice is from twelve to twenty inches thick. If you have leisure, a trip on one of the excursion or regular line of boats constantly plying up and down, cannot fail to give you abundant satisfaction. Scattered through the whole course of the stream are numerous islands, from one to several thousand acres in extent. Their number will average one a mile for the entire length of the river; and for beauty of scenery it is second only to the St. Lawrence.

DETROIT COLLEGE OF MEDICINE.

Neighboring Cities and Resorts.

Several days could be agreeably disposed of among the regions round about Detroit.

A ride of little more than an hour on the Michigan Central, westward, will take you to the beautiful city of Ypsilanti where the State Normal School is located; and less than two hours on the same route will land you at Ann Arbor, where hours may be spent examining the treasures of the University.

In both these cities the hard, smooth roads over hill and moor, along the winding river through lovely scenery will tempt to drives in almost every direction.

Going northwards by the Detroit & Milwaukee Railroad, an hour's ride will take you to Pontiac, the center of one of the most magnificent farming regions in the Union. Here one of the State Insane Asylums is located. A delightful drive of five miles will bring you to Orchard Lake, a most charming summer resort. A first-class hotel, excellent boating and fishing opportunities, delightful drives, and a Military School for boys, are among its attractions.

Two days or more could profitably be given to Put-in-Bay and vicinity, with its beautiful islands, lovely scenery and memorable localities in connection with Perry's victory. Perry's Cave is beautiful with stalactites and crystals of various forms. It is reached by a broad stairway, has an average height of six feet, and is 200 feet long by about 150 feet in width. Here also are fine fishing grounds, with plenty of boats and bait; and in season grapes are very abundant and cheap. It has all the usual accompaniments of a first-class watering place, including good hotel accommodations.

One day, or several, at the Star Island House would afford health and pleasure in abundance. Going up the

ST. JOHN'S GERMAN EVANGELICAL LUTHERAN CHURCH.

river, you stop on a little island at the termination of the St. Clair Flats Canal, and here, at moderate rates, you can fish, hunt and boat to your heart's content.

Taking a steamer from Star Island and passing through Lake and River St. Clair, you will have a view of river scenery that will be fully satisfying.

"The Oakland," a noted hotel near St. Clair, is a favorite stopping place.

Returning to Detroit by the Grand Trunk Railroad and stopping at the village of Mt. Clemens, you may gain health by the use of the water at the Magnetic Springs. There is unquestionable evidence of remarkable cures from the use of this water. A pleasant day can be spent in a trip to Chatham, Canada, which you reach by way of Lake St. Clair and the picturesque River Thames.

An exceedingly attractive resort, known as The Mettawas Hotel, is reached by the Lake Erie, Essex & Detroit River Railroad, running from Walkerville, opposite Detroit, to the coast of Lake Erie, opposite Pelee Island, a distance of only thirty miles from Detroit. Investigation will amply demonstrate its claim to extraordinary attractions as a summer resort.

HOUSE OF CORRECTION.

Wayne County Savings Bank.

This Bank was organized October 2, 1871, under the General State Law. The original capital was $30,000; in September, 1875, it was increased to $150,000. Its first officers and trustees were: W. B. Wesson, President; H. Kiefer, Vice-President; S. D. Elwood, Secretary and Treasurer; W. A. Moore, Attorney, J. J. Bagley, J. Croul, J. B. Sutherland, J. Wiley, M. S. Smith, S. G. Wight, D. M. Ferry, Paul Gies, L. P. Knight, Traugott Schmidt, D. M. Richardson, W. C. Duncan, T. W. Palmer, F. Adams, K. C. Barker, G. F. Bagley, J. S. Farrand, and D. Knapp.

The Bank was established at No. 101 Griswold Street, on the northwest corner of Congress Street, but within two years these premises became too small, and as no suitable offices could be rented, the Directors, in September, 1875, increased the capital to $150,000, and decided to erect a building for the use of the Bank. The lot, 50x132 feet in size, on Congress Street West, just in the rear of their first location, was procured, and a building erected at a total cost of $110,000. It is known as Nos. 32 and 34 Congress Street West, and was first occupied on December 15, 1876.

There is only one other Bank in Detroit that owns its bank building, and that the Directors made a judicious and economical investment is evidenced in the fact that the Bank has not only been amply accommodated at a cost of several thousand dollars a year less than poorer facilities would have cost, but the property has increased in value nearly $50,000 over the original investment.

W. B. Wesson served as President until his death, and S. D. Elwood, who had been continuously Secretary and Treasurer, then became President. Jacob S. Farrand, who had served many years as Vice-President, after his death in 1891, was succeeded by D. M. Ferry.

RESIDENCE OF SUPERINTENDENT OF HOUSE OF CORRECTION.

The Trust, Security and Safe Deposit Co.

This company is connected with the Wayne County Savings Bank, and has its offices and vaults in the same building. It was organized in 1872, with a capital of $30,000.

The first officers were W. B. Wesson, President; Jerome Croul, Vice-President; S. D. Elwood, Secretary and Treasurer; William A. Moore, Attorney; John Collins, in charge of vaults; and, although nearly twenty years have elapsed, the officers have remained unchanged, except that Mr. Wesson has passed away.

It may accept and execute any trust created by an instrument in writing which appoints it as trustee, and receives from any individual or corporation, on deposit, for safe keeping and storage, gold and silver plate, jewelry, money, stock securities, and other valuable papers or personal property. The corporation may also become security for administrators, guardians, trustees or persons, in cases where, by law or otherwise, one or more sureties are required, at such rate of compensation and upon such terms and conditions as shall be established by the directors.

Terms Per Year of Special Deposits.

Government and other coupon securities, or those transferable by delivery, including bank bills,	$2 00 per	$1,000
Government and all other securities, not transferable by delivery,	1 00 "	1,000
Gold coin or bullion,	1 25 "	1,000
Silver coin or bullion,	2 00 "	1,000
Silver or gold plate, under seal, on owner's estimate of full value, and rate subject to adjustment for bulk, on a basis of	1 00 "	100

VIEW OF END OF THE SERIES OF VAULTS.

VAULTS AND ENCLOSURE.

INSIDE OF THE IRON AND STEEL VAULT.

Jewelry and precious stones, $2 50 per $1,000
Deeds, mortgages, valuable papers generally, } 1 00 a year each, or
when of no fixed value, } according to bulk.
Wills for life, $5 00; per year, $1 00

Safes inside the fire and burglar proof vaults can be rented at $10 to $75 per year.

Collection and remittance of interest or dividends, on bonds or stocks, 1 per cent. on amount collected.

For collection of other income and management of property, special rates.

No charge less than one dollar.

The Safe Deposit Company's Vaults.

The vaults, four in number, occupy a portion of the first floor in the fire-proof Wayne County Savings Bank building, and are entirely independent of main walls of same, with ample passageway all around for the night and day patrol.

In their construction, no expense was spared to make them as positively fire and burglar proof as money and the skill and ingenuity of the best manufacturers and mechanics could erect.

The foundation is solid masonry and concrete. The walls of the vaults are five feet thick, built of best quality brick, laid in cement, and every course tied with strips of iron.

The brick walls are lined inside with railroad iron, each rail being securely fastened with strong screws. Inside the rail the vaults are lined with alternate layers of steel and iron, three inches in thickness, fastened by conical bolts, with heavy nuts inside. The steel plates are so prepared that they are positively drill proof, retaining toughness and ductility that render them equal proof against the sledge and wedge. The steel plates are bent at right angles, securely binding the corners. The vault doors are secured by Sargent's combination and chronometer locks.

LITTLE SISTERS' HOME FOR THE AGED POOR.

HISTORY

OF

DETROIT AND MICHIGAN.

By SILAS FARMER,

HISTORIOGRAPHER OF THE CITY OF DETROIT,

(By Appointment under Ordinance of 1883.)

Member of American Historical Association, Webster Historical Society, Michigan Pioneer Society, etc.

It contains 1,072 pages, in double columns, quarto form, with 648 illustrations, consisting of fac-similes of a variety of Old Records, Documents, Hand-bills, Noted Localities, representations of Seals, Monuments, Banners, and relics of various kinds, together with a large number of maps and plans.

In range of subject and fullness of treatment, it is the most complete local history published in America. **Fully one-third of the volume is devoted to matters that relate to Michigan in general, and the information is new and singularly interesting.**

In every library the list of volumes on Michigan and Detroit is particularly meagre; this history will amply fill this want, and as a work of reference, no other volume can take its place.

Over ten years of labor were spent upon this work, no expense was spared in its preparation, and it unfolds a large amount of authentic and surprising information hitherto unpublished and unknown.

It is printed on seventy pound supersized and extra highly calendered paper, and is elegantly bound in genuine Turkey morocco, with cloth sides and appropriate tool work in gold.

Published in one volume at **$10.00,** or in two volumes, with additional biographical matter, at **$15.00.**

GROTTO OF THE VIRGIN, ON GRATIOT ROAD.

COMMENDATIONS.

Justin Winsor, Librarian of Harvard University, Corresponding Secretary of Massachusetts Historical Society, and Editor of the "Narrative and Critical History of America," on page 622, vol. 5, says, "This is the most important local history yet produced in the West."

From the Army and Navy Register, Washington.

* * * "*Any city in the United States might well be proud of such a historical work as this.*" * * The author has ransacked all the historical collections of the country to obtain facts bearing upon the history of Detroit. He has even had recourse to foreign collections. Some idea of the amount of labor he has put into his book may be gained from his statement that he has received 2,166 letters from correspondents on historical points connected with his work. His preface, giving an account of the authorities selected and the manner in which he has obtained his facts, is, in itself, a remarkable story. * * We sincerely trust there is possible a proper remuneration for the author of such a remarkable municipal history as this. We suppose that only a very live, flourishing, and public-spirited city could produce such a work, which must conduce greatly to the honor and advantage of the city wherever it is seen."

From the Magazine of American History, N. Y.

"The history of a city two hundred years old, or nearly, that has twice been besieged by savages, once captured in war, once destroyed by fire, whose allegience has been claimed by three different sovereignties, and whose flag has changed five times, cannot otherwise than possess a charmed interest for the American people. Mr. Farmer's work seems to have been undertaken in the true historical spirit, and executed with painstaking and conscientious care. * * One notable chapter of thirty pages is devoted to the British and Indian wars, the French and Spanish intrigues, and the war of the Revolution. Another chapter treats of Indian wars from 1790 to 1812; and two chapters (XLI. and XLII.) contain the history of the war of 1812. Mr. Farmer has written this portion of the work admirably, bringing forward *fresh information of priceless value.* * * The preparation of the work has involved more than ten years' persistent and faithful labor, and *it is one of those productions which no library in the country can afford to miss from its shelves.*"

THE POST OFFICE.

From Chicago Legal News.

* * * "The style of Mr. Farmer is pleasing, concise and accurate, all necessary requisites for a historian. The chapters on 'Legislatures and Laws,' 'Justice in the Olden Time," and on the "Supreme Courts of the Territory," show phases of legal affairs in the early days that are duplicated in the history of no other locality, and shown in no other volume. * * In the small space allotted to this review, we are not able to convey an accurate idea of the merits of this valuable work. It should be in every library in the United States."

Farmer's "Detroit." From the Critic, New York.

"It would be well if every growing city would appoint an official whose duty it should be to keep its archives in order and commit to the press such memorials as its citizens might desire to preserve. Taking this judicious view of the matter, the City Council of Detroit in 1842 wisely established the office of City Historiographer. With less evident wisdom they made the office 'purely honorary.' The result was that, as usual, they got as much as they gave. At length, however, with better fortune than this parsimony deserved, the office fell to a public-spirited holder, Mr. Silas Farmer, who has performed its duties as well as if it had been accompanied by a salary—and possibly better. In a handsome octavo volume of a thousand pages he has given us a "History of Detroit and Michigan." * * The contents of the volume comprise everything that the history of an American city should be expected to contain, and the work may well be taken as a model by other civil historians." * *

Boston Evening Transcript.

"If Boston, New York, Philadelphia or Baltimore had such a history of its earlier years, what a treasure would they have * *

"The local information in this book is simply immense, and the manner in which all this information is 'boiled down,' and the method by which it is put together, is truly a marvel. * *

"The position which Detroit held to the great Northwest of a half-century ago makes this book of large interest to all who are studying the formation of the western cities and States, and the growth of the laws peculiar to their respective localities. It has much unpublished and fresh information. * *

"The history of Detroit will never have to be written a second time."

Harper's Magazine, June, 1887.

"Since our national centennial, especial attention has been given by many writers in different parts of the country to the development of local history, and their researches have led to numerous publications of more or less value according to the temper and

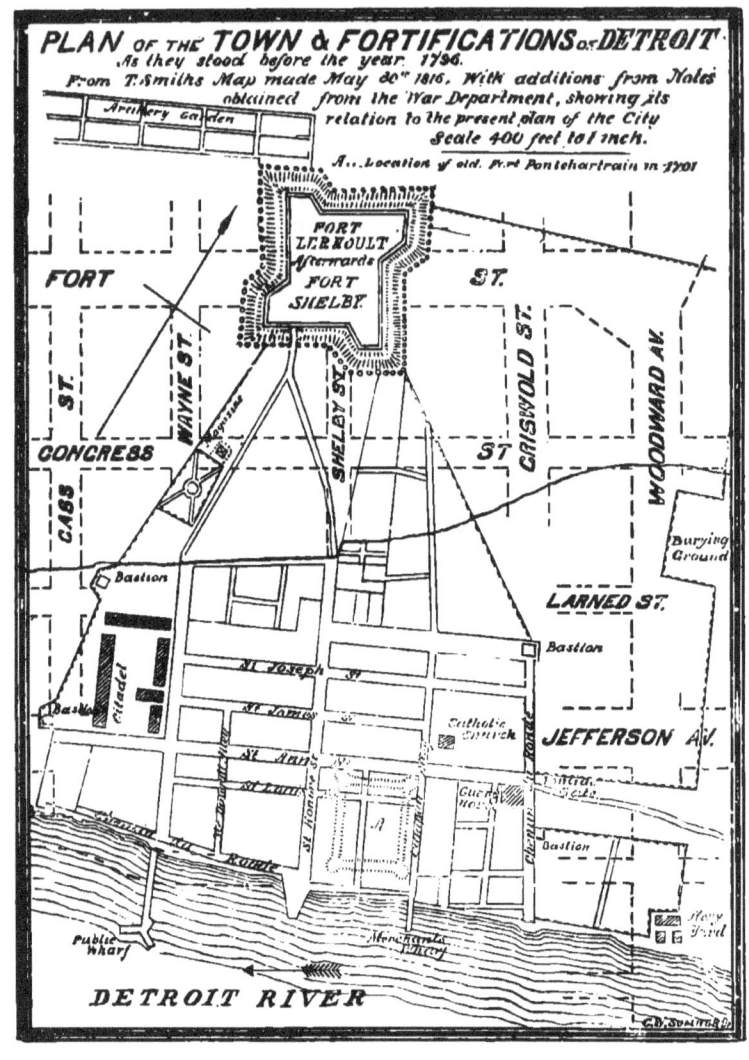

MAP SHOWING GROUNDS OF OLD FORT SHELBY.

industry of the writers. Among the most important as well as the most interesting of these publications is the superb volume prepared by Silas Farmer, entitled *The History of Detroit and Michigan*. The author has brought to his subject not only a mind of rare intelligence, but a soul in love with the Queen City of the Straits. We have here the result of many years' patient, diligent, and painstaking industry; and this is not more admirable than the taste and judgment which have shaped the materials drawn from so many sources into a harmonious whole. The style is simple, direct, and elegant, worthy of a more ambitious work. The scope of the volume is not narrow. In the writer's mind his narrative 'epitomizes the history of half a continent.' Only here can be found any adequate view of the early history of Michigan. * * The completeness of the work is astonishing. The author has not only exhausted the rich materials to be found in published works; he has gathered much that is interesting from an extensive personal correspondence with men who possessed in one shape or another unpublished materials; he has not only utilized numerous old French letters, documents, and manuscripts, but has instituted special inquiries in France, especially in connection with the career of Cadillac; and he has ransacked not only all the documentary reports and correspondence bearing upon his subject, but also the old files of local newspapers in various parts of the country. * * It need not be said that such a work is not only a history but a cyclopœdia of Detroit and of the Territorial history of Michigan. It can be said of no fact relating to the subject to be found in any other work, that is not found here, and it contains a rich store of material that cannot be found elsewhere. Every writer upon the subject, since Mr. Farmer's book was published, not only could find here everything he might wish to know, but, if he would be assured of accuracy as to details and dates he must consult this book. * * A work that must stand forever as the most complete book of reference on all matters concerning the early history of Detroit and Michigan."

SEND FOR CIRCULAR.

ADDRESS,

SILAS FARMER & CO.,

31 Monroe Avenue,

DETROIT, - - - MICH.

FORT STREET PRESBYTERIAN CHURCH.

CEMETERY MAPS

WITH

Lists of Lot Owners and Numbers.

PUBLISHED BY

SILAS FARMER & CO.

PRICES:

Mount Elliott............................	$1.00
Elmwood...............................	1.50
Woodmere.............................	1.50

Nine Cemeteries once existing within the present City of Detroit are now obliterated, and there is no full record of the lot owners in any one of them, nor any record to show who was buried therein.

In the official registry of lot owners in some cemeteries of the present day, the names of lot owners are often misspelled, frequently no surname is given, the locations of the lots as given therein do not always agree with the location given in the deed, and in more than one instance the records themselves have been stolen or mutilated.

Some lots in certain cemeteries now have a value of several thousand dollars, and yet there is no evidence of title on record in any City or County Office, and deeds given to individuals are frequently lost.

Hundreds of families in Detroit have no evidence as to where their parents or grand-parents are buried, and many who are interested in genealogical researches (and all ought to be) would pay a large sum to know where their ancestors lie. The present generation should remedy this evil as far as possible, and those who follow should have such a record as can now be obtained and preserved.

The evidence afforded by such a register as is here given, will often be of value as a clue in settling titles to property, aid many persons who do not easily find their lots, and become an increasingly valuable historic record, as the changes of time obliterate monuments and recollections.

ST. ANNE'S ROMAN CATHOLIC CHURCH AND SCHOOL.

THE TEACHER'S TOOL CHEST

A 36 page Tract, in a handsome cover, with many illustrations, is designed for either Sunday School or Day School Teachers. It is suggestive, inspiring, and helpful. Price, six cents each, or in lots of ten or more, five cents each, postage paid.

ADDRESS, **SILAS FARMER & CO.,**
31 Monroe Avenue, corner Farmer St., Detroit, Mich.

COMMENDATIONS.

From Rev. Warren Randolph, Pastor Central Baptist Church, Newport, R. I.

Silas Farmer, Esq., Detroit, Mich.

DEAR SIR.—Your ingenious "Teacher's Tool Chest" brings out many most important truths, and in a way which will doubtless fix them in minds from which they would slip if presented in the ordinary—perhaps we may say, prosaic way. You certainly have hit upon an original idea. Yours very truly,
WARREN RANDOLPH.

Editorial Rooms, Department of Sunday Schools and Tracts, Methodist Book Concern, New York.

Mr. Silas Farmer, Detroit, Mich.

MY DEAR FRIEND. —I have taken great enjoyment in examining your little book "The Teacher's Tool Chest." I find it quaint, suggestive, interesting and profitable. Any teacher who will read its hints and follow them, will be a better teacher thereby.
Sincerely yours, JESSE L. HURLBUT.

Boston, Mass.
"Thanks for a copy of 'The Teacher's Tool Chest.' The tools seem to me of excellent steel and admirable patterns.
JOSEPH COOK."

From M. C. Hazard, Editor of Publications of Congregational Sunday School and Publishing Soc'y, Boston.

"Calculated to arouse and stimulate teachers."

From Rev. Joseph Estabrook, Superintendent of Public Instruction of Michigan.

"I have looked it through with care and interest. It pleases me very much, and I can see how it can be made very useful."

From Rev. E. W. Rice, D. D., Editor Publications of American Sunday School Union, Philadelphia.

"It is ingenious, bright, suggestive, and immensely helpful to the busy teacher."

WINDMILL POINT IN 1888, LOCATED BETWEEN WHAT IS NOW SWAIN AND CAMPAU STREETS.

The Drinker's Dictionary

This is a work of sixty-eight pages, with an entirely new, original and humorous illustration on every page.

It is instantly attractive to both old and young, and is a valuable addition to any Sunday School Library.

It is pungent, pathetic and powerful.

Price 10 cents in paper, or 30 cents in cloth cover with gilt stamp, postage paid.

Thousands of copies sold.

Special rates to the trade or by the hundred.

ADDRESS,

SILAS FARMER & CO.,
DETROIT, MICH.

This little book is a very remarkable work and in an original (o-rye-gin-ale) way defines many of the words in a liquor drinker's vocabulary, and each definition is illustrated by a telling cut, de-sign-ed and en-grave-d especially to warn all people concerning the "true inwardness," meanings and personified effects of what these terms represent. The entire book is pun-gently written, and its hard hits are often tenderly tipped with scriptural texts of fire, that point the swiftest road to hell or the surest way to heaven. Although so sharp, decisive and incisive, as many of its paragraphs are, yet they are full of pity, piety, sweetness and a Christian desire to help, and to cure all whom they may wound. There is in its composition such a blending of wit, oddity, wisdom, learning, satire, Christianity, deep feeling, and good will, by means of a quaint, juggling and plasticity of word-handling, accompanied by pictures so comical, yet so impressive and expressive of the dire calamities and degradation of a drunkard's career that the reader don't know whether to laugh or cry; still the whole is ballasted with Bible passages so pleasantly and properly put in that he realizes through them, there is not only "saving grace" for the drinker, but for the reader also. It will do every person many times its cost worth of good to become the possessor of a copy of this odd, peculiar, unique publication. Every page has its picture, its puns, its pity and piety, and there is not one of them all (there are 64 in number,) but what is worth far more than the whole costs. We heartily commend it for its novelty and much more for its real merit.—*From "The Sixteenth Amendment," Buffalo.*

ST. LUKE'S HOSPITAL AND CHURCH HOME.

THE TRUTH TELLER.

Our tract with the above title contains twenty pages, in the form of a **Newspaper**, and is thoroughly unique.

It treats of **60** different subjects, mostly in Bible language, has a number of illustrations, and will be preserved by every one as a literary and religious curiosity.

It is a valuable compendium of gospel truth, and is full of "**seed thoughts.**"

Price 3 cents each, or $2.50 per hundred, postage paid. Send for specimen. Address,

SILAS FARMER & CO., DETROIT, MICH.

The "TRUTH TELLER" is the most ingenious and striking arrangement of scripture texts we have ever seen.—*Union Signal, Chicago.*

THE ROYAL RAILROAD.

The Fiftieth Thousand of this tract is now issued. It has thirty-six pages, and a picture on every page, and is printed on fine paper, with enamelled paper cover; stitched.

"I have found all classes and grades of men receive it kindly, while they would not look at an ordinary tract." T. F. JUDD, *Y. M. C. A. R. R. Sec'y.*

"It is excellent and original." FRANCES E. WILLARD, *Pres. Nat. W.C.T.U.*

We have hundreds of testimonials as to its interest and value.

It is sent anywhere, postage paid, for 3 cents each, $2.50 per 100, or $10 per 500.

On orders for 100 or over, any notice will be printed on back of cover without extra charge.

Address, **SILAS FARMER & CO.**, Detroit.

Maps of Detroit and Environs

Size, 20 × 24 inches, pocket form, 25 cts.; mounted, 50 cts.

Size, 45 × 55 inches, mounted, $6.00.

Sectional Maps of Michigan
AND ALSO OF
Lake Superior Region.

Size, 24 × 36 inches, pocket form, $1.50.

Address, **SILAS FARMER & CO.**, Detroit, Mich.

WILLIAM BRIGHAM WESSON, late President of the Wayne County Savings Bank, was born in Hardwick, Worcester County, Massachusetts, March 21, 1820, and was the son of Rev. William B. Wesson, who for many years was pastor of the Congregational Church of Hardwick.

Mr. W. B. Wesson's connection with Detroit dates from the year 1833. He came when a lad of thirteen with his brother-in-law, the late Moses F. Dickinson. In 1841, he entered the literary department of the University at Ann Arbor, and was subsequently admitted to the bar. His attention, however, was almost immediately attracted to the possibilities connected with the real estate business, and he soon formed a partnership with Albert Crane, and they became pioneers in the business of subdividing large tracts of land and disposing of the lots, and were the first to sell lots upon long time, with only a small payment down. His investments, however, were not wholly in the line of real estate, and he found time to engage in various public enterprises. He was for several years President of the Detroit, Lansing & Howell Railroad, and aided materially in securing its completion, and it may be stated, as a remarkable fact, that his services were rendered to the company for a series of years without drawing the salary attached to the office, and he declined to receive any pay for his services. He was also prominent in the building of the Grand River and Hamtramck street railroads. He served as President of the Wayne County Savings Bank and of the Safe Deposit Company from the organization of these corporations until his death in 1890. He was also President of the Detroit Safe Works, and a director and large stockholder in the First National Bank.

In 1872 he was nominated for State Senator, and although the district was strongly Democratic, he was elected by a large majority, carrying every ward and town in the district. As State Senator he proved so useful a friend to the University that the faculty, without his previous knowledge of their purpose, conferred upon him an honorary degree.

WILLIAM B. WESSON.

JACOB S. FARRAND, late Vice-President of the Wayne County Savings Bank, was born in Mentz, Cayuga County, New York, May 7, 1815. His parents came to Detroit in May, 1825, but after a few months removed to Ann Arbor. While living at Ann Arbor, Mr. Farrand, then a boy of thirteen, carried the mail on horseback between Detroit and his home. Two years later, in 1830, he came to Detroit, where he secured employment in the drug store of Rice & Bingham. After six years' service, having attained his twenty-first year, he formed a partnership with Edward Bingham, and embarked in the drug business, continuing therein almost continuously until his death in 1891. His active energies were also directed to other business channels, where equal success followed his endeavors. For many years he was Treasurer of the Detroit Gas Light Company; a Director of the Detroit Fire and Marine Insurance Company; Vice-President, and from its organization a Director, of the Wayne County Savings Bank; from the beginning connected with the Michigan Mutual Life Insurance Company, and for many years its President. For years he was also a Director of the First National Bank and was its President from 1868 to 1883, holding the position at a time when able financial management and the full confidence of the people were especially needed. His wise counsel, good judgment and far-seeing ability, as well as his personal worth, inspired the fullest trust in all the institutions under his control.

From 1860 to 1864 he was a member of the Common Council. During this period he served for one year as President of the Board and for a short time was acting Mayor. When the Metropolitan Police law was enacted he was appointed Police Commissioner for the long term, and served eight years, all the time as President of the Board, after which he was solicited to continue in office, but declined a re-appointment. For twenty years he was a member of and served as President of the Board of Water Commissioners. He ever evinced a warm interest in educational projects, and as a member of the Board of Education was for several years a helpful factor in securing liberal provisions for the maintenance of public schools.

JACOB S. FARRAND.

ENTRANCE TO WOODMERE CEMETERY.

OFFICERS

OF THE

Wayne County Savings Bank

1891.

S. DOW ELWOOD, - - - - President.
D. M. FERRY, - - - - Vice-President.
WM. STAGG, - - Ass't Sec'y and Treasurer.
WM. A. MOORE, - - - - - Attorney.

DIRECTORS.

THOMAS W. PALMER.	D. M. FERRY.
WILLIAM A. MOORE.	JEROME CROUL.
H. KIRKE WHITE.	FRANCIS ADAMS.
E. H. FLINN	L. P. KNIGHT.

S. DOW ELWOOD.

SUGGESTIONS.

SUMS AS SMALL AS $1.00 received from any person, and a Bank Book furnished without charge.

MARRIED WOMEN and Minor Children may deposit money so that no one else can draw it.

SOCIETIES may deposit money from time to time, and, before making the first deposit, may provide by vote how and by whom it shall be drawn out; and, provided a copy of the resolution is furnished to the Savings Bank, no money will be paid, unless its provisions are strictly complied with.

MEANS FOR IDENTIFYING DEPOSITORS.—When a new depositor first comes to the Savings Bank, precautions are taken and records made, so that he may always be identified, and in case a book is lost, the owner thereof cannot be defrauded.

PERSONS RESIDING OUTSIDE the City of Detroit, who may wish to deposit money of their own in the Wayne County Savings Bank, or the funds of Estates, Heirs, Minor Children, or Trust funds of any kind, can do so in person, or by remitting to the Bank by Express, Draft, P. O. Order, and a Certificate of Deposit or Bank Book can be returned; and, under the rules of the Bank, the money cannot be withdrawn, unless the owner is identified in person, or has given proper authority for others to draw the same.

All transactions with this Bank are strictly confidential.

BANKING HOURS.—9 o'clock A. M. until 3 o'clock P. M. Saturdays, in the evening from 6 to 8.

THE CASINO, BELLE ISLE PARK.

REPORT OF THE CONDITION

OF THE

WAYNE COUNTY SAVINGS BANK

AT

DETROIT, MICH.

AT THE CLOSE OF BUSINESS, MAY 4, 1891.

RESOURCES.

Loans and discounts	$1,372,173 65
Real estate, loans	1,055,919 94
Invested in bonds	2,169,946 08
Due from banks in reserve cities	746,194 90
Banking house and lot	110,000 00
Furniture and fixtures	6,625 12
Other real estate	37,137 58
Current expenses and taxes paid	16,181 47
Premium paid on bonds	10,425 82
Collections in transit	2,261 36
Checks and cash items	26,191 04
Nickels and pennies	258 04
Gold	50,090 00
Silver	2,648 60
U. S. and national bank notes	40,580 00
Total	$5,647,481 55

LIABILITIES.

Capital stock paid in	$ 150,000 00
Surplus fund	150,000 00
Undivided profits	310,972 00
Savings deposits	5,032,859 15
Premium and exchange	580 40
Foreign exchange	15 00
Rent account	3,054 98
Total	$5,647,481 55

State of Michigan, County of Wayne, ss.

I, Wm. Stagg, Assistant Treasurer of the above named bank, do solemnly swear that the above statement is true to the best of my knowledge and belief.

WM. STAGG, Assistant Treasurer.

Subscribed and sworn to before me this 11th day of May, 1891.

CHARLES F. COLLINS, Notary Public.

Correct—Attest:

H. K. WHITE.
S. DOW ELWOOD, } Directors.
D. M. FERRY,

OCCUPATIONS AND NATIVITY OF DEPOSITORS IN THE WAYNE COUNTY SAVINGS BANK, JANUARY 1, 1891.

OCCUPATIONS OF DEPOSITORS.

Agents, 723.
Auctioneers, 11.
Actors, 32.
Architects, 21.
Artists, 32.
Barbers, 237.
Brewers, 32.
Butchers, 331.
Bookkeepers, 723.
Baggage Masters, 43.
Boiler Makers, 248.
Blacksmiths, 614.
Basket Makers, 21.
Barkeepers, 54.
Brokers, 10.
Bakers, 238.
Brush Makers, 88.
Bricklayers, 89.
Bootblacks, 93.
Broom Makers, 64.
Bankers, 72.
Builders, 76.
Bill Posters, 53.
Brakemen, 72.
Bookbinders, 97.
Brass Founders, 10.
Carpet Weavers, 53.
Clerks, 3,733.
Carriage Makers, 65.
Copper Smelters, 54.
Collectors, 96.
Confectioners, 32.
Contractors, 54.
Conductors, 259.
Chair Makers, 84.
Carpenters, 2,600.
Cashiers, 21.
Cigar Makers, 1,050.
Carriage Trimmers, 54.
Coppersmiths, 32.
Capitalists, 33.
Carvers, 31.
Coachmen, 11.
Coopers, 129.
Carriers, 140.
Cooks, 43.
Clergymen, 27.
Cabinet Makers, 291.
County Treasurers, 21.
Dentists, 25.
Draymen, 97.
Dressmakers, 32.
Deputy Sheriffs, 21.
Druggists, 248.
Doctors, 334.
Draughtsmen, 32.

Detectives, 13.
Drovers, 6.
Dyers, 10.
Dairymen, 11.
Engineers, 658.
Editors, 118.
Engravers, 21.
Farmers, 2,602.
Florists, 13.
Firemen, 129.
Finishers, 140.
Foremen, 37.
Grocers, 356.
Gardeners, 280.
Horsemen, 6.
Hotel Keepers, 151.
Hatters, 64.
Housemovers, 4.
Hucksters, 32.
Harness Makers, 75.
Housekeepers, 22.
Hostlers, 43.
Inspectors, 10.
Infants, 752.
Jewelers, 97.
Junkers, 21.
Justices of Peace, 32.
Janitors, 32.
Journalists, 27.
Lawyers, 248.
Lumber Dealers, 162.
Laborers, 3,164.
Laundrymen, 73.
Librarians, 21.
Lithographers, 53.
Letter Carriers, 32.
Lamplighters, 8.
Locksmiths, 10.
Merchants, 753.
Mining Engineers, 8.
Milkmen, 10.
Messengers, 75.
Musicians, 86.
Mechanics, 1,076.
Machinists, 742.
Masons, 345.
Millers, 108.
Manufacturers, 162.
Molders, 529.
Ministers, 172.
No given occupation, 5,199.
Newsboys, 64.
Notaries, 10.
Opticians, 10.
Organ Makers, 75.
Painters, 452.

OCCUPATIONS OF DEPOSITORS—Continued.

Printers, 700.
Plumbers, 183.
Pattern Makers, 65.
Plasterers, 172.
Policemen, 129.
Peddlers, 177.
Porters, 97.
Paymasters, 10.
Photographers, 65.
Perfumers, 11.
Roofers, 21.
Railroad Men, 291.
Real Estate Dealers, 43.
Reporters, 15.
Rectifiers, 10.
Servants, 399.
Sail Makers, 63.
Sewing Machine Operators, 21.
Surveyors, 22.
Sailors, 653.
Stereographers, 10.
Shoemakers, 781.
Stationers, 13.
Superintendents, 21.
Saloon Keepers, 280.
Students, 775.
Stone Cutters, 205.
Societies, 302.
Stewards, 21.

Saddlers, 43.
Steamboat Men, 32.
Switchmen, 37.
Sawyers, 43.
Trunk Makers, 43.
Tinsmiths, 322.
Tobacconists, 111.
Tailors, 450.
Teachers, 302.
Tanners, 237.
Teamsters, 268.
Trustees, 10.
Telegraph Operators, 210.
Treasurers, 43.
U. S. Army, 280.
Upholsterers, 172.
U. S. Navy, 43.
Varnishers, 21.
Watchmakers, 65.
Wagonmakers, 118.
Wood Sawyers, 21.
Watchmen, 75.
Wood Turners, 65.
Whitewashers, 21.
Waiters, 73.
Wire Workers, 97.
Wood Dealers, 21.
Women, 13,706.

NATIVITY OF DEPOSITORS.

America, 23,979.
Germany, 18,047.
Ireland, 5,506.
Canada, 4,022.
England, 3,096.
Nova Scotia, 21.
India, 21.
Finland, 43.
Wales, 84.
France, 454.
Scotland, 1,670.
Poland, 511.

Unknown, 1,221.
Russia, 43.
Switzerland, 603.
Belgium, 151.
Sweden, 86.
Bohemia, 216.
Denmark, 86.
Cuba, 21.
Italy, 108.
Holland, 302.
China, 32.
Japan, 2.

Foreign Exchange and Letters of Credit.

The Wayne County Savings Bank issues Bills of Exchange (of sterling or francs), payable in the following cities on as favorable terms as can be obtained in the United States. No charge beyond the cost of same to parties who keep accounts with this Bank:

Alexandria.	Dundee.'	Luzerne.	Pisa.
Amsterdam.	Dusseldorf.	London.	
Aachen.	Dresden.	Leghorn.	Rotterdam.
Athens.		Lisbon.	Rome.
Algiers.	Edinburgh.	Luxembourg.	
	Erfurt.		Stirling.
Belfast.		Manchester.	Strasburg.
Basle.	Florence.	Marseilles.	Stuttgart.
Berne.	Frankfort.	Mayence.	Schweinfurt.
Baden-Baden.		Metz.	St. Petersburg.
Bayreuth.	Glasgow.	Moscow.	Saarbrucken.
Berlin.	Geneva.	Milan.	Stockholm.
Bremen.	Gottingen.	Mannheim.	Seville.
Brunswick.	Genoa.	Magdeburg.	Smyrna.
Bonn.		Madrid.	
Brussels.	Havre.	Munich.	Trieste.
	The Hague.	Malaga.	Turin.
Cork.	Hanover.	Malta.	
Carlsbad.	Heidelberg.		Venice.
Cassel.	Hamburg.	Nice.	Vienna.
Coblenz.		Naples.	
Copenhagen.	Innsbruck.	Nuremberg.	Worms.
Cologne.			Wiesbaden.
Carlsruhe.	Jerusalem.	Oldenburg.	
Christiania.			Zurich.
Constantinople.	London.	Paris.	
Cadiz.	Liverpool.	Palermo.	
	Leith.	Prague.	
Dublin.	Lyons.	Pesth.	

and six hundred other towns and cities.

We offer our services to all parties who intend going abroad, or who wish to make remittances, and can give all desirable information as to the sailing and arrival of ocean steamers, and a list of European correspondents, in whose care letters to travelers may be addressed.

We issue letters of credit payable in Great Britain, the Continent and the East upon the most favorable terms, accepting bonds or other securities as collateral.

www.ingramcontent.com/pod-product-compliance
Lightning Source LLC
Chambersburg PA
CBHW020111170426
43199CB00009B/493